EARLY REVIEWS OF P~

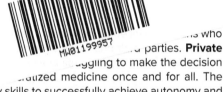

Dr. Grace Torres-Hc ...s who want to reclaim the ... parties. **Private Practice Solution** wi ...ggling to make the decision to escape the bonds ...auzed medicine once and for all. The reader will gain the necessary skills to successfully achieve autonomy and avoid costly mistakes. If you want to enjoy practicing medicine again, I highly recommend reading this book.

Ellen W. McKnight, MD - Rheumatology
Owner, Summit Arthritis & Infusion

This visionary book explores the untapped potential direct care medicine offers specialists and surgeons in terms of patient-centricity, cost-effectiveness, and individual freedom. Dr. Grace has written a must-read for anyone seeking transformative solutions in healthcare.

Christopher Habig
Co-founder & CEO, Freedom Healthworks
Host, *Healthcare Americana* Podcast

Private Practice Solution is an invaluable guide for physicians looking to take back control of their private practice. Dr. Torres-Hodges masterfully unveils strategies for reestablishing autonomy by examining the profit centers in your practice. With a clear focus on empowerment, the book outlines actionable items that allow doctors to focus on the doctor-patient relationship and provide excellent care to their patients.

Michele N. Kurlinski, DPM - Podiatry
Owner/Founder, Lighthouse Foot & Ankle Center

True change will only come when physicians refuse to participate in the broken healthcare system. I urge every physician to return to self-ownership and rediscover the real joy in medicine: the physician-patient relationship. Read Dr. Grace's book to learn how easy opening your own direct practice can be.

Rebekah Bernard, MD - Family Practice
Owner/Founder, Gulf Coast Direct Primary Care

I have experienced many benefits from having a direct care medical practice (third-party free) - benefits both for patients and for physicians. Among the many personal benefits, the most surprising one is the greater degree of happiness that comes from practicing medicine once all of the bureaucratic nonsense is filtered away. I work for my patients and no one else. I am only responsible to my patients, not the government, a hospital, or an insurance company. I enjoy practicing medicine more now than ever, and because of that I don't think I will ever retire. A private, direct care practice is the best way to preserve the integrity of the medical profession and the sacred patient-physician relationship. If that's what you are looking for, **Private Practice Solution** is a great first step in that direction.

Gerard Gianoli, MD - Otolaryngology
Owner/Founder, The Ear and Balance Institute

It's no secret that patients have made Direct Care among the fastest growing practice models in modern medicine, and there's no better example of why that is than Dr. Grace's own story. The book is a blueprint for the future of medicine.

Richard W. Walker
Executive Director, Benjamin Rush Institute

As we continue to see Direct Primary Care (DPC) explode, the next step is to expand the direct care model into the specialty arena. Patients need specialty care options outside of the insane insurance system. This book lays the groundwork for physicians to overcome their fears, build a plan and start their own direct care practice. A must-read.

Shane Purcell, MD - Family Practice
Owner/Founder, Direct Access MD
Founder, DPC Alliance

Other doctors told me that Direct Pay Dermatology wouldn't work. They said, "people won't see you if they have insurance". They were wrong. It's a business model that works, if you do it wisely, and that's what **Private Practice Solution** is about. But, the challenges of the direct pay model are not what keep physicians from doing it; it's that they think they can do better in the conventional model. My message to physicians who are in third party payer-based medicine is that many of you think you can win this game. The rules keep changing, and you keep adapting. But, in the long run, I don't think you can win if you are working for an unethical corrupt boss or bosses. That is because your patients aren't winning. You may rationalize your decisions and you may practice self defense, but patient autonomy and choices are continually eroded. It may be very difficult for you to get out of third-party payer-based medicine because of your need for equipment and personnel. However, if you see that your patients don't get all the choices that you would want if you were them, that you don't really work for them, and most importantly that you can't be fully honest with them, you should try to get out.

Kathleen Brown, MD - Dermatology
Owner/Founder, Montana Dermatology

It's no secret that our third-party payor system is in shambles. Not only are sky-high premiums and red tape hurting patients' financial health, physicians are being hurt, as well. This isn't healthcare. The constraints of today's "sick-care" system mean doctors can only be reactive in the short office visits, rather than health-focused proactive. Dr. Grace experienced this; the bureaucratic red tape and increasing loss of autonomy. She looked for – and found – a better way. Read her **Private Practice Solution**, follow the plan, approach your practice as you would another patient, and you can comfortably transition into running a successful, direct care, cash pay practice... and love it!

Jim Grapek
Co-host, *Cash Patient Free Market* Podcast
Founder, ThePavilionCenter.com

Drawing from my personal journey as a direct care rheumatologist, I've witnessed profound growth and a transformative shift in my mindset and approach to medicine. Dr. Grace Torres-Hodges' latest book illuminates the path for physicians seeking to practice medicine on their own terms and foster deeper connections with patients. By distancing oneself from constraining metrics and third party contracts, physicians can reacquaint themselves with the genuine essence of medical practice, cultivating an environment where passion thrives and the sense of purpose is rekindled. Alongside Dr. Grace, the Direct Specialty Care Alliance is steadfast in its mission: to empower physicians with the tools and knowledge to reclaim their professional autonomy.

Diana Girnita, MD, PhD - Rheumatology
Owner/Founder, Rheumatologist-on-Call
Co-founder, DSC Alliance

I am so glad to hear about this book by Dr. Grace Torres-Hodges! Every day AAPS receives more and more calls from patients seeking the name of an independent doctor who will put the patient first. Patients are simply not receiving the personalized care they desire from the medical professionals who are constrained by insurance companies, hospitals, and government red tape and dictates. Simultaneously we are hearing from more and more physicians who tell us about how these entities are interfering with their capacity to treat patients with their best judgment and to the fullest extent of their ability. So, there may never be a better time than now for physicians to explore launching an independent practice to help serve the increased demand of patients seeking high quality, affordable, individualized, medical care. If you are a physician, in any specialty, who is considering independent practice, or have ever dreamed about it, do not miss this opportune time to make the dream a reality.

Jeremy Snavley
Business Manager, American Association of Physicians & Surgeons

Direct Care private practice models put the doctors and patients back in the center of the healthcare industrial complex (Patient-Centric Care) unlike the current fee-for-service system where the patient is merely a "target" for profit. Dr. Grace Torres-Hodges' **Private Practice Solution** brings needed guidance and insight into how a physician can have their life back and have a business built around their lifestyle instead of having medicine running your life and leading to burnout. This book is a must read for any physician unhappy with the way things are for it illustrates there can be happiness in medicine and a much better way to take care of patients again!

Carl C. Schuessler, Jr.
Co-Founder & Managing Principal, Mitigate Partners

Dr. Torres-Hodges has captured her experience with such detail that you find yourself gradually nodding more and more until you reach the end and find yourself filled with inspiration, fueled by the expert advice and strategies shared in this book. This is a must-read for any physician who is yearning for autonomy and also the time that they personally determine they need to take care of their patients.

Maryal Concepcion, MD - Family Practice
Owner/Founder, Big Trees MD
Host, *My DPC Story* Podcast

Doctors have to take care of themselves to take care of their patients, and it is increasingly obvious that private practice is not viable in today's third-party payor system. **Private Practice Solution** is a comprehensive guide to understanding your current situation and launching your direct care practice. In doing so you will not only restore your love of medicine and the integrity of the work you are doing for your community, you will also be playing your part in a broader transformation that is happening within healthcare

Zak Holdsworth
CEO, Hint Health

As we watch further consolidation of physicians under the control of large hospitals, and private equity, it is becoming critically important to create a pathway for physicians to escape. Eventually, as it has many times in the past, the pendulum will swing in the opposite direction where physicians will find themselves suddenly needing to recreate a new care-delivery paradigm. For over a decade, we have taken the initiative to work on this on three fronts. We have worked on the supply side, the demand side, and the regulatory side. We have created a grant-supported training pathway to teach physicians how to start and be successful in a direct-care model. We have created an educational outreach where we reach the general public to teach them how and why they should seek out care through direct-care practices. Finally, we sought to create a regulatory environment that was friendly at the state and federal level to nurture and protect direct-care practices. Through these efforts and many of those such as yourself, there is a safety net for physicians that choose to make the leap and jump to safety. The future of our profession and our patients depends upon it. Thank you, Dr. Torres-Hodges, for adding another important tool for this transition!

Lee Gross, MD - Family Practice
Owner/Founder, Epiphany Health DPC
Chairman, DPC Action
President, Docs4PatientCare Foundation

PRIVATE PRACTICE

solution

RECLAIMING PHYSICIAN AUTONOMY AND RESTORING THE DOCTOR-PATIENT RELATIONSHIP

GRACE TORRES-HODGES, DPM, MBA

EDITED BY SUSAN J. PATNAIK

Dedicated to My Family

To my children, Tim & Caitlyn, who endured countless recounting of my transition story with doctors and who were my biggest cheerleaders by encouraging me to simply "Write the book, Mom!"

and

To my dear husband, Michael, for truly saving me by seeing the path to direct care medicine before I did and helping me navigate through the transition. He deserves to hear his 3 favorite words from me - "You were right!"

Contents

INTRODUCTION

"Those in pursuit of WHY are inspired to do what is right. Our passions are ignited when we set out to advance a cause greater than ourselves. Fulfillment comes when we do something to help someone else. When we know WHY we do what we do, everything falls into place."
- **Simon Sinek**, author of *Start with Why* and
The Infinite Game

Private practice physicians today are experiencing unprecedented levels of stress due to outside interference from third-party players. This interference is negatively impacting the care their patients receive and the financial performance of their practices. What's even more troubling is that the situation seems to only be growing worse year after year. This raises an obvious question: just how much stress can a private practice physician endure before enough is enough?

I reached my limit several years ago. Fed up with the third-party payor system and all the hoops I had to jump through to keep my practice going, I set out to find a new way of practicing—one that honored my autonomy as a doctor and honored the sanctity of my relationship with my patients.

A few years after deciding enough is enough, I now no longer accept insurance in my practice. All services are cash-pay only. This business model is known as Direct Care (Direct Pay) private practice. In my opinion, Direct Care Medicine is the best solution to the madness currently plaguing private practice physicians. It completely eliminates third-party interference by eliminating third-party payors. It's a simple concept but getting there is not a simple process.

I wrote **Private Practice Solution** to share the wisdom I gained along the way as I transitioned from an insurance-based private practice to a purely cash-based one. There was no guide for me to follow when I set out on my mission. I had to learn through trial and error. This book is a collection of principles, strategies, and tools for any doctor interested in coming over to the other side with me. My hope is that it will serve as a guide for doctors who want to take action but don't know where to start.

Your interest in this book tells me you are interested in Direct Care Medicine. That you want to reclaim your autonomy as a physician. That you want to gain financial freedom from a broken healthcare system. More importantly, it tells me that you are ready to take a big step toward professional freedom—the freedom to provide your patients with high-quality medical care unencumbered by bureaucratic interference. That is a big deal!

Although, at times, you might feel alone in your thinking, I can assure you that you are not alone. Rather, you are one of a growing number of physicians who are bucking the system. You are a free-market thinker, and you are on your way to becoming an amazing Direct Care doctor.

So, take a moment and give yourself credit for arriving at this pivotal point on your professional path. Acknowledge the courage, forethought, and hard work it takes to not only forge a new path but to seek proper guidance along the way.

But, before you go full-on, let me warn you of a hazard ahead. Enthusiasm for this bold new venture can easily get overtaken at some point by fear of the unknown. As questions trickle into your head, they can quickly turn into a flood, which can then cause you to freeze up and the excitement to fizzle—and open the door to doubt. It's like any other challenge. There is an inside game to be played, a mental game. And you need to be ready.

Whether you are a seasoned physician wanting to transition your traditional insurance-based practice to a Direct Care model or you are a newly graduated resident looking to launch a Direct Care private practice from the get-go, you're very likely wrestling, at the very least, with a few basic questions such as:

- *How will patients find me if I'm not in their insurance network?*

- *How do I set my prices and communicate them to my patients?*

- *Will patients really pay out-of-pocket for my services?*

And, if you are a specialist who has heard only of Direct Primary Care (DPC) and nothing beyond that, perhaps you are asking:

- *Does this model actually work for specialists?*

It's not surprising. Working within the insurance-based (third-party payor) system, you are shielded from basic market dynamics that other business operators face on a day-to-day basis. And so, given your distance from the money side of medicine and the conditioning you've received for years if not decades, these questions can leave you feeling unnerved, as well they should, because they can't be answered from within the confines of your current perspective.

The fact is, practicing Direct Care Medicine requires a major shift in mindset, something that is easier said than done. How can such a shift come about if you've never been exposed to the new mindset in question? It's something of a *Catch-22*, isn't it?

That's why I decided to write this book. I feel like the best thing I can do for you—a physician on the threshold of this great venture—is to fly straight into the storm that is likely brewing in your mind, calm the turbulence, and then slowly and steadily provide you with the information you need to develop the proper mindset and toolkit for a successful Direct Care practice.

This book is designed to help you understand why you might be experiencing mental blocks such as analysis paralysis and how you can overcome them. It's designed to help you unlearn old ways of thinking that are no longer valid in the new realm of Direct Care Medicine. It is designed to empower you to be intentional in your thinking and decision-making as you map out a cohesive plan—a plan built on a solid foundation of pricing, positioning, and branding, the three keys to successfully marketing your Direct Care practice.

I am Dr. Grace Torres-Hodges, a board-certified podiatrist and foot surgeon, the owner/founder of Torres Hodges Podiatry, a Direct Care specialty practice located in Pensacola, Florida. In 2013, amidst the onset of changes initiated by the Patient Protection and the Affordable Care Act (aka PPACA or ACA), I attended a meeting by the American Association of Physicians and Surgeons (AAPS). The conference theme was "How to Thrive Not Just Survive." It was there that I met like-minded physicians who invited me to consider free-market medicine by suggesting I drop contracts with third-party payors.

My break from the system didn't happen overnight. All told I participated in the third-party payor system for over 15 years—since I first started my private practice in 2001. But by 2017, for the first time in my career, I had fully opted out of ALL third-party contracts, including Medicare. I transitioned to be 100% insurance free.

So, you see, it was not that long ago that I was in your same shoes—sick and tired of being mistreated by the system but, at the same time, rather daunted by all the unknowns ahead of me. I remember feeling concerned, uncertain, and unsure of myself. I remember wondering *How am I going to do this?*

What-if scenarios haunted me. *What if my patients balk at my new policies? What if they leave me? What if I have to close my practice?* I was worried not only for myself but also for the staff who depended on me.

But I didn't let all those thoughts get the best of me. I didn't let them put me in retreat. Instead, I kept reminding myself **WHY** I was leaving the insurance model, and then I tapped into those reasons to fuel my momentum while step-by-step, I launched my Direct Care practice and freed myself from the headaches of the insurance system—a system, which was limiting my potential to provide the best care for my patients.

And since doing so, I have had many wonderful opportunities to pay it forward by advising other physicians on doing the same, specialists of all backgrounds, including

- A general surgeon in the Carolinas, who was let go by a hospital during Covid.

- A cardiologist in Georgia whose group was bought by an equity firm.

- A PM&R specialist in New Jersey, who needed help setting cash-pay rates.

- An oncologist in Wisconsin seeking guidance on selectively dropping certain third-party payors.

And, of course, as a podiatrist, I've mentored fellow Foot & Ankle specialists across the country, from Maine to California, who were looking to work smarter, not harder, and wanted some shortcuts for transitioning to Direct Care Medicine.

As you start reading this book (no matter what kind of internal battle you might have going on) please know this: **You are absolutely capable of building a Direct Care practice**—one that is successful, profitable, and satisfying, one that provides you autonomy over both your professional and personal life.

But I'll be honest, to build a successful Direct Care practice, **you must first build a Direct Care mindset**. Changing one's way of thinking comes easier to some than to others. We all develop blinders of one sort or another over time. However, simply knowing that you **can** change your mindset, that you **can** remove blinders, and that all this is completely **within your power**– is the first step in making the shift. Whether or not you decide to do the work to build a Direct Care mindset–it's completely up to you.

For example, have you ever wondered why it is so difficult for doctors to define their value in monetary terms? As doctors, we can talk to people about extraordinarily difficult life-and-death matters from diabetes to cancer, but when it comes to compensation for our services, we tend to clam up and become like a "deer in headlights."

Or we change the conversation altogether to avoid those feelings of awkwardness. To help you build a Direct Care mindset, I will walk you through this unique struggle we doctors deal with, as well as the history of our profession's relationship with third-party payors and our reliance on **others** to set our rates and thus define our worth.

Before I can help you identify your value proposition within the free-market system and build a Direct Care practice, you **must** first pull back the curtain and take a close-up look at the game you, as an insurance-based medical practitioner, are currently engaged in. You must understand how the rules of the game evolved and accept the challenge to grow and learn!

This might feel a little uncomfortable for you, but there's nothing to fear. It's not as if we doctors haven't faced and overcome many uncomfortable situations on our journey through medical school and residency. Discomfort, as we all know, is a part of growing, and that's what is required to expand your mindset beyond the conditioning you received both in medical school and as a doctor who was paid through the third-party reimbursement system.

Shifting from insurance/third-party payor medicine to Direct Care Medicine is exactly that: **a SHIFT**. It will require you to rethink and reorient your approach to offering medical services to patients. This book aims to help you make that shift by serving first as a guide and roadmap for building a Direct Care mindset so you can then move on and do the work of building an amazing Direct Care practice.

After you clear this mindset hurdle, you'll feel your internal resistance fade and the steps required to build your Direct Care practice will seem more natural and intuitive. After all, when you boil it down, managing a Direct Care practice is mostly based on common sense logistics and mathematics. You already have the intellectual aptitude to run a business (that includes creating a marketing strategy and pricing system for your services.) You simply have to use those cerebral muscles in a slightly different way than you are used to. Trust me: it will not be more difficult or complicated than anything you've already done in your career. In fact, I think you might discover it's actually rather simple.

This book has been divided into four sections.

- Section One: Understanding the Situation

- Section Two: Analyzing Your Current Practice

- Section Three: Making Decisions

- Section Four: Launching Your Direct Care Practice

I have found it helpful for many of my clients to think of their practice as a sick patient. I would ask them, "How would you approach any other patient that might come to you for help?" The answer oftentimes follows the standard SOAP note: take a history, perform an examination, diagnose the condition, and then create a treatment plan. Well, this is what we are going to do in this book. You will start by gathering the history of your patient's condition, next you will examine your patient using the Key Performance Indicators (KPIs), after that, you will diagnose your patient (does it need to be treated?) and, finally, you will create a treatment plan for your patient.

Let's look at all the ways in which a medical practice could be considered *sick*:

- **Financial Health**: When a practice has bills it must pay, when a practice has a payroll it must meet, when a practice has a mortgage payment it must cover, that practice needs a predictable stream of cash flow coming in to remain solvent and financially healthy.

But when the conversion of accounts receivable into liquid cash is unknowable and unpredictable and the payor of those accounts is beyond accountability, that's a recipe for fiscal sickness of the practice, not to mention a source of immeasurable stress on the doctor.

- **Patient Experience**: Your practice exists to serve patients. So if your practice is suffering, then you can be sure your patients will suffer right along with it. When doctors are stressed, fatigued, and bogged down with unmanageable levels of bureaucratic paperwork, they are not able to provide the best care for their patients. Patient-centered care and personal attention go out the window and are replaced with rushed exams. The patient is then at greater risk of poor medical care, their doctor's focus having been hijacked by concerns that are at odds with the patient's needs. We might as well add the financial woes of your patients to our list. Financially stressed patients have limited resources to spend on their health care and are often not able to make ideal choices for their treatment. Increasing premiums and higher deductibles lead to financial strain on your patients which leads to financial strain on your practice.

- **Physician Autonomy**: Physicians have lost autonomy over the treatment of their patients. An army of middlemen has sprung up in the form of bureaucratic regulators and inserted itself between doctors and patients. Their administrative regulations compromise doctors' judgment. They are, in effect, barriers to proper treatment: a maze of authorization requirements doctors must navigate; a series of circus hoops they must jump through before they can proceed with the treatment of their patients. In a healthy practice, physician autonomy would not be questioned. Doctors would not be ordered to perform bureaucratic acrobatics or have to beg for permission to give their patients the care they need. Loss of physician autonomy is a clear red flag that your practice is sick.

- **The Doctors' Mental and Physical Health**: Stress is a killer! Aren't we doctors the ones who came up with that PSA? But now, what are we doing? We're allowing ourselves to be stressed to death. **Stress** from longer hours. **Stress** from increased patient volume. **Stress** from chaos in the flow of our practices—the delay in office visits as well as those being scheduled. **Stress** from trying to keep up with charting to the point of having to take it home and work on it after hours. **Stress** from the fear of making an error as we are rushed through patient exams, leaving us less and less time to interview our patients, examine them, and discuss their conditions. Where does this all end?

There you have it. A definition of your patient. And a breakdown of your patient's symptoms. Your practice is your patient, and now it's up to you to save your patient.

As the famous line from *Hamlet* goes, "Something is rotten in the state of Denmark." Medical practices have been warped under the strains placed upon them by the third-party payor system, and it doesn't feel healthy at all. Why? *Because we are rushed and we end up treating patients reactively rather than proactively.*

And what do we call our profession? We call it "healthcare." Oh, the irony!

In what way and on what planet does our practice of medicine qualify as "healthcare?" If we are being honest with ourselves, and with our patients, we would call what we do "sick-care." Because let's face it, that's what it amounts to—responding to and treating sickness. NOT promoting health.

You may be feeling rather down about your ability at the moment to provide first-rate care to your patients. But here's the cool thing: you have the ability to turn things around by first taking care of your practice. If you make your practice your patient, if you accept that it is unwell and you create and follow a treatment plan to restore it to health, you will eventually have a practice where "health-care" (not "sick care") is what you actually offer, not just say you offer. And your patients will thank you for it.

As you continue reading, know that you are not alone in trying to figure this puzzle out. Every doctor I've mentored and even I, myself, have struggled with feelings of trepidation and self-doubt as we've moved forward, one jagged puzzle piece at a time, until the picture became clear and coherent.

I'm happy to report, these brave doctors—though they may have wanted to from time to time—did not throw up their hands in defeat and walk away from the profession they loved. They didn't let the madness of the system push them out of medicine. No. They learned to work smarter. They hung on to a steadfast conviction that they did indeed possess the skills and intelligence necessary to build a successful Direct Care practice. And after much worthwhile effort, they continued to practice medicine using a new model of doing business and found joy in their work again. And you, my friend, can do the same!

It's time for doctors to take back the narrative!

It's time for doctors to reclaim physician autonomy and regain control of their careers!

I hope you will join me and the many others who have taken the leap and never looked back. You now hold a guide in your hands to help you along the journey.

LET'S GET STARTED!

SECTION 1

UNDERSTANDING THE SITUATION

"It's ironic that the federal government already has a mandatory disclosure rule for the real out-of-pocket costs people incur at a vulnerable time in their lives. But it's not a rule for health care—it's for funeral homes. The Funeral Rule, 18 enacted by the Federal Trade Commission in 1984, requires funeral providers to offer itemized pricing information to consumers before they purchase any services."
— **Dr. Marty Makary**, surgeon, public policy researcher, and author of *The Price We Pay*

Think about what goes through your head when you encounter a new patient—before you hear those first few familiar words, "Doc, I've got this problem…" The moment you crack the door, enter the exam room and see your new patient for the first time, your mind goes right to work taking a history.

You scan your patient from head to toe. You notice the demeanor, mannerisms, and facial expressions. You even notice how your patient is dressed. Neat? Disheveled? In those five seconds, before either of you has said a word, you've already gathered a great deal of information.

Then, as the conversation unfolds, you continue to pick up on subliminal details: your patient's response time to questions, speech patterns, and inflections, the volume of the patient's voice, breathing, and eye movement. Some of these details are obvious. The big things. Some are less obvious. The small things. Those small things can be equally as significant as the big ones, if not more so. My point is, you know instinctively to stay alert and to watch for both the big and the small. This is all part of gathering the patient's history.

Ok, then. That's what we are going to do in Section One. We're going to go over the history of your practice's condition as if it were a patient. As we do, I want you to take note of the giant glaring issues as well as the ones hiding out of plain sight. I want you to pay attention to subliminal clues. I want you to challenge cursory answers and remain open to new interpretations.

In doing so, you will be using the same diagnostic skills you use when treating your patients. But, in this case, I want you to use these skills to spot crucial signs and signals of dysfunction within our profession and your practice and to observe the trends that have led to this dysfunction and illness.

As you will see when you read through the chapters in Section One, it wasn't one big thing here or there—but rather the cumulative effect of all the little things—that made your practice sick. ***Understanding how we got into this mess will be essential to understanding how we get out of it.***

By the end of Section One, I hope to have opened your eyes to two phenomena:

1. How the system is working against you—the independent physician—in favor of larger and larger bureaucracies.

2. How your mindset is working against you in the form of past conditioning.

Only then, with eyes wide open, will you be ready to embrace the task at hand: moving forward with your goal of building a successful Direct Care practice.

CHAPTER 1

SO, WHAT'S GOING ON?

Exchanging Independence for Dependence

In 2016, the business magazine *Forbes* ran an op-ed piece predicting "the death of the private practice doctor's office."[1] The article placed blame for the demise of private practice medicine on federal policies, specifically those linked to the ACA. This act of federal legislation created financial incentives and regulatory requirements that reward large organizations for consolidating with others into even larger organizations while at the same time, they penalize smaller, private practice outfits. Through basic carrot-and-stick measures, federal policies have been motivating the powerful to become more powerful and making life difficult for anyone who dares to remain independent—so difficult that the small independents are starting to give up and shut down.

In theory, these policies were meant to bring about a greater good. They were supposed to lower overall healthcare costs and improve overall healthcare outcomes. However, the results so far are mixed and do not support the premise.

The same *Forbes* article identified a second (and related) trend: an ongoing decline in the number of independent physicians as a percentage of the total population. In 2008, **62%** of all doctors were independent. By 2014, the propor-

---

1   Reed, Wilson "Why Private Practice Is Dying." Forbes, September 7, 2016. https://www.forbes.com/sites/realspin/2016/09/07/why-private-practice-is-dying/.

tion had dropped to **35%**. The article referred to this phenomenon as a "stampede." Doctors, it said, are exchanging independent status for employment positions – or dependent status - with healthcare enterprises in record numbers.

Fast forward a few years and we see this trend shows no sign of slowing down. In 2021–*Year Two* of the COVID-19 pandemic–the exodus of physicians from private practice to institutional employment continued. Keep in mind that in 2020 and 2021 there was an explosive rise in buyouts of private medical practices by hospitals. According to *Becker's ASC Review*, as of April 2022, there were approximately 135,300 hospital or corporate-owned physician practices in the U.S. Of that number, 36,200 (or roughly 27% of the total) had been acquired in the previous two years, a seismic increase.

At the beginning of 2022, nearly **74%** of all physicians identified themselves as *employed*, leaving a mere **26%** of physicians practicing independently.[2]

So, what we are witnessing here is a rather rapid reorientation of the healthcare landscape with physicians trading in professional independence for professional dependence at an alarming rate, seemingly unaware of or indifferent to the fact that once the handcuffs get locked in place, they are nearly impossible to remove.

How Does This Affect the Consumers of Healthcare?

Take a moment to consider how this trend impacts the consumers of healthcare services or, as you know them, **your patients**. In 2008, a patient had more independent doctors to choose from than that same patient in 2014. In 2008, for every 100 physicians practicing medicine, 62 of them were independent practitioners. In 2014, that num-

---

2   Dyrda, Laura. "Private Practice Physicians Drop to 26%." Becker's ASC Review, April 20, 2022. https://www.beckersasc.com/asc-transactions-and-valuation-issues/private-practice-physicians-drop-to-26.html.

ber was 35. In 2022, it was only 26. From 2008 to 2022, that's a 61% decrease! What a blow to consumer choice!

How Does This Affect You?

What do you feel when you read these statistics and predictions? What do you feel when you hear that powerful forces are pressuring smaller players to hand over their keys and fall in line? Does it feel like a rug is being pulled out from under you? Think of those who are in medical school or residency right now. Is independent private practice even on their radar? Is it even a viable option? Do thoughts like these make you feel discouraged? Defeated? Fearful?

It's easy to see why hospitals and big corporations would cheer this trend away from private practice medicine and independence. It's easier to place administrative requirements, productivity requirements, and quality standards on doctors who are employees as opposed to doctors who are independent practitioners. Who knows if the corporate entities intentionally set out to dominate physicians and keep them firmly under their control? Or if they were merely responding to government incentives logically? It doesn't matter what their intention was. What matters is where we find ourselves at this point.

An Interesting Twist

So, here's the deal. *Forbes* isn't wrong. Private medical practices are closing or selling out to corporate buyers and, on the whole, are declining in number. And an increasing number of physicians are opting for the financial security of employment within organizations rather than remaining in their current insurance-based private practice. If you focused on nothing but these two trends, it would be easy to feel defeated.

However, **there is more to the story**. There is a third trend.

Among the doctors who have decided to remain in private practice, *Forbes* discovered something fascinating: **more and more private practice doctors are abandoning third-party payor-based business models and shifting to cash-based models instead**. In other words, there is a silver lining here—a third trend—and that is the rise of Direct Care Medicine.

And can you guess what is driving this trend? Think about it. It is the administrative policies and changes pushed and enacted by third-party payors: both those in the government as well as those in the private sector.

Unsustainable Pressures

Forbes isn't the only one to make this connection. The Journal of *Medical Economics* makes the same claim based on feedback from the doctors they interviewed.

In a nutshell, more and more doctors are calculating the costs of providing care within the third-party payor system and deciding that the costs outweigh the rewards. It's just not worth it anymore. Simply put, doctors are growing sick and tired of the administrative hassles that come with managing their practices.[3] And these hassles, they report, are only getting worse with each passing year due to the implementation of seemingly endless incentives—each one followed by an assigned penalty.

Add to that the burden of keeping up with annual changes in forms, coding, and EMR linked to Affordable Care Act initiatives. Bureaucratic changes such as these result in more busy work for doctors, thereby fueling their frustration with the system.

---

3   "The Rise of Direct Primary Care." MedicalEconomics, April 10, 2016.
https://www.medicaleconomics.com/view/rise-direct-primary-care.

Doctors in insurance-based private practices are more dissatisfied than ever with the status-quo insurance model. They want to spend more time with their patients and less time doing paperwork, but they feel like the tide is going against them.

As the level of depression and burnout among physicians rises to new heights, you see doctors starting to give up on the profession. Some have left medicine for good, retired early, or switched careers. Sadly, too many of us know of someone practicing medicine who has succumbed to a deep level of despair, and we are all aware of the increased risk and rising rate of physician suicide.

That said, there is a hopeful number of doctors—and this number is growing—who are not giving into the pressure to fold but rather are digging in and forging a new, healthier, empowered path forward. And thus, the rise of the Direct Care model of practicing medicine.

What Do Patients Want?

Despite the ever-shrinking population of independent physicians and private medical practices, we see consumer demand for medical care from this breed of doctor GROWING, not declining. In September 2022, a headline on *Yahoo News* read "Demand for the Direct Care Healthcare Model Continues to Grow".[4]

Why would that be? Why would demand for services from Direct Care physicians be on the upswing when the number of physicians in private practice is shrinking? It might seem contradictory, but only on the surface. If you take a deeper look, consumers of healthcare are looking for alternatives to the status quo for the same reasons

---

4   Sergay Dermatology "Demand for the Direct Care Healthcare Model Continues to Grow." PR Newswire: press release distribution, targeting, monitoring and marketing, September 23, 2022. https://www.prnewswire.com/news-releases/demand-for-the-direct-care-healthcare-model-continues-to-grow-301632087.html.

doctors are looking to shake up the status quo: they are fed up with all the hassles!

Patients Are Rational Actors

It's easy to get lost in the physician's perspective. But don't forget you are a consumer, too! You have been a patient yourself at some point, and when you remember those experiences, you should be able to relate to the frustrations patients feel these days with a healthcare system that isn't prioritizing their needs.

The amount of time it takes to resolve a health issue within the insurance framework continues to increase. From making an appointment to getting a referral to checking on authorization to waiting for results to making another appointment just to obtain the results—the cycle of delay after delay is becoming more and more wearisome.

And that doesn't even take into account the patient's experience in the doctor's office. A patient might wait up to 40 minutes or longer to get a mere seven minutes of time with the doctor. Sitting in a packed waiting room with the doctor's schedule clearly overbooked, patients can't help but feel like they are being run through a conveyor belt. Even more common these days, the patient isn't guaranteed to see the same physician from one visit to the next, or a physician at all. Many visits are completed by a nurse practitioner or a physician assistant.

What happened to the sanctity of the doctor-patient relationship? What happened to personalized care?

Furthermore, patients today are asking why they are paying higher health insurance premiums while ALSO paying out more in deductibles and coinsurance. That doesn't make much sense. *Where is the money going?* they wonder. *And why are physicians retiring early and leaving medicine?*

Patients, like all consumers, are pretty sharp, and the equation is not adding up. They sense they are losing something of value without gaining anything of value in return. Insurance-based healthcare is feeling more and more like a losing proposition: pay more in time and money and get less and less in exchange.

Patients were noticing changes as an explosion in the growth of health administrators was occurring. A study completed at Harvard reported that between 1975 and 2010 the number of physicians grew 150%, roughly proportional to population growth.[5] However, a study by Athena Health following the implementation of the Health Insurance Portability & Accountability Act (HIPAA) and ACA in 2010 reported growth in healthcare administration of **3,000%.**[6] Yes, you read that right!

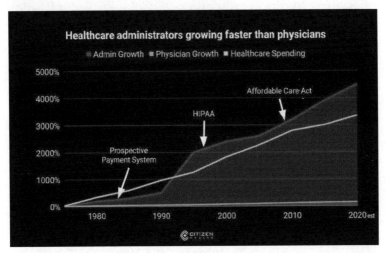

with permission by John Chamberlain, MHA, LFACHE - Citizen Health

5   Chandrashekar, Pooja, and Sachin H Jain. "Understanding and Fixing the Growing Divide Between Physicians and Healthcare Administrators." The Journal of Medical Practice Management, March 2019. https://www.proquest.com/docview/2504870463.

6   Carr, Brian. One reason for rising health care costs is growth in the number of hospital administrators, March 12, 2020. https://www.dallasnews.com/opinion/commentary/2020/03/15/one-reason-for-rising-healthcare-costs-is-growth-in-the-number-of-hospital-administrators/.

Administration is important, but there is no healthcare without doctors. Patients want doctors, not red-tape administration.

Alignment of Interests

What I hope you are beginning to understand is this: **the essence of clinical medicine is (and always has been) centered on the doctor-patient relationship**. And doctors and patients are lining up in agreement on that principle, especially now that it is under growing attack. The more bureaucratic the healthcare system becomes, the more individuals in both groups (doctors and patients) are considering opting out of the standard way of doing things and looking for new, more effective solutions—new paradigms if you will. And the decision by many independent physicians to stop contracting with insurance companies is turning out to be a win-win proposition.

Just consider how the pandemic impacted medical care. When the rest of the world shut down and kept people away, Direct Care practices remained open with little disruption in care for their patients. You can't say the same for institutional practices. That's merely one example of how the Direct Care model has served the interests of both parties.

Another factor to consider is the small business community. The ACA federal mandates require businesses with 50 or more employees to offer health insurance. The need for small businesses to keep costs down has led them to investigate the benefits to their employees, as well as their own bottom line, of Direct Care Medicine.[7]

---

7   "Small Business and the Affordable Care Act (ACA)." Small Business and the Affordable Care Act (ACA) I HealthCare.gov. Accessed January 14, 2023. https://www.healthcare.gov/small-businesses/learn-more/how-aca-affects-businesses/.

Small businesses that cannot afford traditional health insurance for their employees can provide important, comprehensive primary care for their employees at a fraction of the cost. Other, innovative methods of paying for health care services incorporate Direct Care Medicine into their product offerings. Staggering costs are forcing businesses to innovate. It's good for them as well as for their employees.... your patients![8]

So, let me return to the previous question: Why would demand for services from Direct Care physicians be growing when the overall number of physicians in private practice is shrinking? It comes down to three factors:

- More private practice doctors are transitioning out of insurance-based medical models and offering their patients a more desirable level of care.

- Patients are becoming savvy consumers of healthcare and learning how to shop for the best providers. They are looking for providers who have the time and freedom to help them solve their problems quickly and efficiently. Remember, time is money, and health is wealth. Money is not the only factor consumers consider when making a decision.

- Employers are discovering the cost-saving benefits of including Direct Care options in their health plans.

---

8   Hint Health. "Trends in Direct Primary Care 2022."

CHAPTER 2

HOW THE HECK DID IT GET SO BAD?

Everyone Has a Story: Here's Mine

I'll be honest: I had to get kicked around a little first before I became interested in the history of our third-party payor system. As you well know, they don't cover this subject in medical school. So, like many others, I entered the profession wearing rose-colored glasses, assuming that my patients would always get the care they needed and that I would always be fairly compensated for the care I provided.

But by 2013, practicing medicine had become increasingly frustrating for me. And I felt compelled to take a close look at the situation. I wanted to figure out what I was missing.

You see, I started my practice, like most of you, treating my patients and writing up the SOAP notes in paper charts. I still remember having to learn how to use EMR (electronic medical records) for the first time. It was during my first job after residency. There was a small learning curve, but I type fast and tend to be a quick study with technology, so it actually wasn't that much of an adjustment.

However, year after year, things changed as government regulators kept coming up with new metrics (quality assurance measures) to analyze. With each new analytic they added to the EMR, one more template or checkbox showed up in the system. And that, of course, meant more for me to address.

In the beginning, these so-called "quality initiatives" sounded somewhat reasonable, even though let's face it, what they amounted to was someone looking over my shoulder. The early initiatives weren't that difficult to incorporate into my day-to-day routine; however, as time went on, some of the check-box questions I was asked to answer had absolutely nothing to do with the actual condition I was treating. No clinical relevance whatsoever. They amounted to little more than data input on my end for the sake of data gathering on the other end.

Like many of you, the sense of burnout I was beginning to feel didn't have anything to do with my patients. I enjoyed medicine. The day-to-day clinical experience was not a grind for me, because every patient who came through my door represented a new puzzle to solve. And I thrive on that type of challenge. More importantly, the relationships I build with my patients (and oftentimes their families, too) as I help them get better and am able to make a difference in their lives—energizes me. And thank goodness it did, because that was the only thing that was keeping me going at the time.

So, I had the existing administrative burden of running a private practice, and that was already taxing enough. Then, thanks to the new quality metrics, I got saddled with this whole new growing level of administrative minutiae that had absolutely nothing to do with the clinical care I was providing patients—MY patients, not THEIR patients. To say it was getting tiresome is an understatement.

Then it began to throw off the day-to-day flow in my office. What do I mean by that? Well, these new administrative requirements created a great deal of uncertainty and disruption. It takes time to look up codes and complete check boxes on the templates. The time it took my staff to perform these functions was time they weren't able to give to the patients. This, naturally, affected the overall patient experience in my office, as patients had to wait longer to be checked in and then again to be brought back to exam rooms and then finally to be checked out. The time that should have been spent focused on the patients had to be redirected to administrative tasks.

Throughout the day, my own flow was also being thrown off—by one disruption after another. If a member of my staff finally got an insurance representative on the phone (after waiting on the line for who knows how long) they had no choice; they had to call me away from whatever I was doing at the moment to have a sidebar or else lose the opportunity to resolve the billing issue in question.

Typically, the staff member would need me to approve or change a particular patient's care plan so it would align with what the insurance company had authorized. These disruptions typically came at the expense of the patient I was seeing at the time. The current patient would be struck there (what choice did they have?) waiting for me while I stepped out and took care of administrative issues for another patient.

Then there was the peer-to-peer discussion many insurance companies would require. I don't know what could be worse than this. Yes, these requirements represented another demand on my time, but even worse than that, the peer-to-peer discussion was often just downright insulting. The peers assigned to authorize my order were typically not in my specialty, and many were not surgeons, yet these peers were the gatekeepers standing between my patients and the medical care they needed.

The bottom line was this: treating patients had become far more complicated than I felt it should have been. When seeing a patient, I had to keep my eye on two balls at all times—the patient and the patient's insurance plan. First, there was the clinical work of creating a treatment plan, deciding upon a procedure, ordering a test, or making a referral. This is what I, as a doctor, was trained to do. And this is the value I bring to my patients. But then there was also the work of figuring out how to navigate the insurance plan to secure coverage for the patient and reimbursement for me while avoiding all the stumbling blocks along the way. I wasn't trained in the minutiae of insurance systems, but I had to learn it (and keep up with it as it changed over time) in order to remain in practice. It was like I was doing two jobs at once.

All this extra work resulted in overbooked schedules in the office. It resulted in hours after work catching up on the things I couldn't do earlier during the patient visit. I began to do charting at home, which, of course, cut into family time. I think what bothered me the most was the violation I felt of my professional autonomy—and the fact that **I was essentially allowing it to happen**. By contracting with third-party payors (like insurance companies), I was granting these non-doctors permission to be in the exam room with me and my patients, and I was allowing them to interfere in relationships I held sacred.

When *Medical Economics* came out with its survey asking doctors "What is running medicine?", an overwhelming majority (70%) said ***third-party interference***. Eureka! Looking back now, it seems so obvious!

Then one day, in the midst of my daily grind, an email popped up in my inbox from the American Association of Physicians and Surgeons (AAPS). It was an invitation to a seminar on "How to THRIVE, not just SURVIVE." I was more than primed for this message. Before long I was learning that I had options available to me that I had never considered before.

Fortunately, doctors are innate problem solvers, and a number of them (also feeling frustrated and burned out) had already started working on solutions to the problems we were all experiencing. Many of these solution seekers were primary care physicians.

Having been hit hard by certain measures associated with the Affordable Care Act, primary care physicians were particularly motivated to opt out of the insurance model. It was the Direct Primary Care (DPC) movement that first proved that the cash practice model could be a viable option for private practice doctors. As the DPC practices began to flourish, other specialists took notice and started exploring similar options.

That's how much most of us really love what we do. Rather than back down in the face of despair, these innovative doctors rolled up their sleeves and worked hard to figure out a new way forward. It's this deep passion for the medical profession that gave rise to Direct Care Medicine!

In retrospect, I feel like there was some force specifically targeting me in those days, trying to get me to wake up. I say this because my life as a doctor had pretty much become a day-in and day-out struggle against individuals and institutions that had no business interfering in my office or in the operating room. And this struggle was relentless. After wasting lots of time banging my head against the wall in frustration, I finally woke up and connected the dots.

In my case, there wasn't one single "straw that broke the camel's back." There were many!

It's one thing for the system to hinder MY decision-making. I was willing (albeit, begrudgingly) to go along with that. But when the system began to interfere with MY PATIENTS' decision-making, that got me going. I could not stand by and let my patients' clinical care be jeopardized. Once this started happening, that's when I knew it was time to get out and find another way to provide care to people, I felt deserved better.

Here are some examples of the type of obstacles my patients encountered–

Something I see daily is an ingrown toenail. I've treated many in my practice, and it's not uncommon for a patient to have ingrown toenails on both feet, not just on one. The common sense approach would be to treat both feet and all ingrown toenails during one visit. But many insurance plans limit coverage for ingrown toenails to one foot per visit. An insurance company would actually require me to send a patient home and have him come back for a second visit to treat the other foot. I never could bring myself to put my patient through such a nonsensical waste of time. I always addressed both feet and all ingrown toenails in a single visit, knowing I'd have to accept non-payment for part of my services. To me, that was the proper clinical thing to do, even if it wasn't the right thing to do for my business.

Another situation I saw often was something I considered diagnosis-discrimination, for lack of a better term. This is when reimbursement would be approved if and only if the patient had what the insurance company deemed "the right" diagnosis. If the diagnosed condition was anything other than what the insurance sanctioned, it would decline coverage, regardless of clinical necessity. These situations defied all sense of fairness in my mind.

For example, there were many times I saw my patients denied coverage by their insurance plans for durable medical equipment they desperately needed. Denied—purely on the basis of a diagnosis code! Take, for instance, extra-depth shoes and inlays to protect patients from pressure points. Such pressure points, by the way, often lead to calluses, ulcers, infections, and amputations—serious medical issues, which are costly to treat. These shoes are typically covered for diabetic patients. But there happen to be many other reasons—reasons completely unrelated to diabetes—why a patient might need such shoes. A patient might have severe arthritis or foot deformities that commercial shoes cannot accommodate. However, without a diagnosis code for diabetes, such a patient—at risk for the same complications that patients with diabetes face—would not be covered for the remedy. End of discussion.

The dilemmas I faced (and my patients faced) were ridiculous. These situations typically ended up in a classic *either/or* scenario: Either the patient would have to go without treatment OR I would have to "just deal with" not getting paid.

It was my policy back then, when it came to my services, to always work it out in favor of the patient's clinical needs, even when it meant swallowing the cost on my end. In my mind, I had a moral obligation to do so. If I chose otherwise, I would be going against everything in Hippocratic medicine and the tenet of "FIRST DO NO HARM".

But as time went on, a little voice deep in the recesses of my brain began to make some noise. Every time I got backed into a corner and forced to make one of those *either/or* decisions, the voice got a little stronger. Finally, I started hearing this voice clearly. I started listening to what it had to say. As doctors, we pledge to *first do no harm* when it comes to our patients. **"But what about doctors? What about the harm done to them?"** the voice was saying, over and over, every time I backed down and accepted non-payment for my services. Then it dawned on me. *First do no harm* should apply not only to patients. It should apply to doctors, too.

As frustrating and unnerving as my predicament felt back in those days, there was a silver lining in the midst of it all. When our broken system began having a negative impact on my patients, a big opportunity opened up. Once my patients began feeling mistreated by the system in the same way I was feeling, only then was I able to start a dialogue with them about the sanctity of the doctor-patient relationship and what was at stake. Their ears began to open up. Our interests merged and the *David versus Goliath* paradigm took hold. The patients began to see themselves and their doctors as Davids and the system as a not-so-benevolent Goliath.

Wow, was I amazed at how intuitive my patients were when we had these discussions. They understood my situation and empathized with me because they were experiencing the same pressures. Not only did they stay with me after I transitioned to Direct Care, they became my best ambassadors.

The Tangling of the Web

As you read this next section, keep in mind that what I am presenting here is simply a very brief overview of a 60-year history of health insurance in the United States as it pertains to physicians. It is an overview and by no means an in-depth treatment of this complex subject.

Our current system—with all its kinks and convoluted requirements—was not purposefully designed to function this way. If you trace the history of its evolution, you will see that our current state of affairs came about as a result of many incremental changes along the way.

Early on, medical care was a service paid for like any other service. Physicians made their services available to patients like blacksmiths made their services available to people with horses, and payment for medical care was the responsibility of the consumer as it was in any other business transaction. Unlike other professions, however, doctors were known for going out of their way to work with patients when it came to payment terms. It was not unusual for doctors to engage in barter, create payment plans or negotiate prices based in part on the patient's financial circumstances.

A Series of Networks Created

In the 1890s, a few lumber companies in the American Northwest began to hire physicians as employees due to the inherent dangers of the industry and the dearth of healthcare providers in the remote areas where they operated.[9] This was a practical business decision more than anything else.

In 1929, a coalition of hospitals in the Dallas-Fort Worth area banded together and created a simple, straightforward insurance product that would pay for an insured patient's hospital visit. This insurance program was called Blue Cross. As its popularity grew locally, the concept gradually spread throughout the country. Eventually, a similar entity was created to cover physician services. This was called Blue Shield. These two organizations and des-

---

9   Fox, P.D., and P.R. Kongstvedt. "Samples.Jblearning.Com." The Origins of Managed Health Care, 2007. https://samples.jblearning.com/0763759112/59117_CH01_Pass2.pdf.

ignations still exist today and together are a major force in both health insurance and healthcare.[10]

In the mid-1940s, the Wisconsin Medical Society was established in response to the needs of returning veterans from World War II. It offered a simple financial product to help manage the costs of healthcare for the people who had served our country in the war.[11]

World War II played another role in the growth of health insurance in the United States. During the war, employers were placed under a wage freeze by the federal government and thus forbidden from granting raises to employees. In order to differentiate themselves in a competitive job market, employers began to offer health insurance products as a "fringe benefit." This was a way to "give a raise" without increasing salaries, and it proved to be very popular.

These early networks marked the beginning of the modern health insurance industry. The initial impact on physicians was minimal as there were few administrative requirements and little to no impact on clinical decision-making. Whatever the doctor ordered for the patient would get approved and would be covered and reimbursed in full. The doctor's assessment, diagnosis, and treatment proposal were honored and followed, not questioned, picked apart, argued down, or denied.

Health Insurance Becomes an Industry

Things began to change in the 1960s with the creation of the Medicare and Medicaid programs. Under the growth

10   Morrisey, Michael. "History of Health Insurance in the United States." Health Insurance, Second Edition, November 1, 2013. https://account.ache.org/iweb/upload/Morrisey2253_Chapter_1-3b5f4e08.pdf.
11   "Celebrating 75 Years of Caring for Wisconsin!" Celebrating 75 years of caring for Wisconsin! I WPS Health Solutions, 2021. https://www.wpshealthsolutions.com/75/.

of these two programs, the United States government began to insure a significant percentage of the American people and also began spending large sums of money on healthcare services.[12] Consequently, the federal government became, and remains today, the *800-pound gorilla* in the health insurance space.

It is worth noting that the government has never had the resources to administer insurance contracts. The highly technical administrative process of administering insurance contracts is beyond the government's capabilities, therefore, it has always been contracted out to private insurers. As a result, a ripple effect occurred, and many aspects of benefit design and administrative practices showed up in both government and private sector insurance contracts. It is not a coincidence; in case you were wondering.

Enter The Health Maintenance Organization

The history of Health Maintenance Organizations (HMOs) is rather interesting. Kaiser Permanente was the very first HMO. It was established in 1945, well before the HMO Act of 1973. Kaiser Permanente was created to provide for the healthcare needs of Kaiser's shipyard workers and their families in California.[13] It was a novel arrangement at the time in that it combined both the financing and the delivery of healthcare services into one integrated system. Kaiser Permanente emphasized preventive care and the coordination of care as a means of controlling overall costs. It required members to select a primary care physician as their first point of contact for all their healthcare needs.

---

12   "History." CMS.gov, December 1, 2021. https://www.cms.gov/About-CMS/Agency-Information/History.

13   Cutting, C.C., and M.F. Collen. "A Historical Review of the Kaiser Permanente Medical Care Program." Journal of the Society for Health Systems, March 1992. https://pubmed.ncbi.nlm.nih.gov/1288670/.

The cost management efficiencies achieved by Kaiser Permanente attracted the attention of others, and before long more and more HMOs were created with the purpose of offering comprehensive healthcare services at lower cost. Like Kaiser Permanente, these other early HMOs were established to provide healthcare to industrial workers and their families. And they were run as non-profit organizations.

The Government Gets Involved

Several decades after the first HMO came into existence, Congress passed The HMO Act of 1973.[14] This was considered a landmark piece of legislation, as it was the first-time federal rules were established to regulate the delivery, payment, and quality of healthcare within the HMO system. Prior to passing this bill, there was little governmental oversight of HMOs, and HMOs were often criticized for providing substandard care to their members.

The intention behind HMOs was a noble one, but federal regulation of HMOs gravely impacted and forever changed the medical profession. It ushered in a new level of managed care in which costs and efficiency began to trump other considerations when treating patients. Focus shifted from meeting the needs of the patient to creating a labyrinthian system and then policing its every rule such as making sure generic drugs were prescribed rather than name-brand drugs and ensuring the proper primary care doctor authorized a referral.

Another big change that came about as a result of the HMO Act involved reimbursement and payment. Before these new laws came into existence, doctors were typi-

---

14   Office, U.S. Government Accountability. "Implementation of the Health Maintenance Organization Act of 1973, as Amended." U.S. GAO, March 3, 1978.   https://www.gao.gov/products/105122#:~:text=The%20Health%20Mainte-nance%20Organization%20(HMO,establishment%20and%20expansion%20of%20 HMOs.

cally paid service by service. With the rise of HMOs, however, physician compensation methods began to change. These changes varied and could be fairly intricate. However, the net result was significant in this respect: if a physician failed to meet certain quality metrics and/or budget goals, she risked payment for her services. That's right. Payment became linked to compliance with the rules set forth by the HMOs, no matter how nonsensical and time-consuming these rules became. In some instances, capitated plans did away with a fee-for-service payment altogether and replaced it with a set amount per patient per month, regardless of the amount of care the patient required. This was a seismic shift for doctors, and it required them to think about their practice revenues and patient care in a different way.

Monitoring and Oversight Become the Norm

The HMO Act aimed a spotlight on the quality of care provided to patients. The goal was to hold HMOs accountable, to make sure the care they delivered was high quality, and to make sure the patient experience was positive. To achieve this objective, a system of monitoring and oversight became necessary. Coordinated care through professional collaboration also became a priority. Doctors were encouraged to work more closely with other healthcare professionals, like nurses and pharmacists, to provide an integrated treatment plan for the patient.[15]

These new administrative and risk-sharing mechanisms became more sophisticated and commonplace over time. They now appear in some form or fashion in virtually every health insurance policy and physician contract in the market. The lexicon of today's medical practice is now replete with these terms: *prior authorizations, referrals, creating*

---

15   "The History of Health Maintenance Organizations." KFF, May 31, 2023. https://www.kff.org/history-and-mission/.

a "gatekeeper," eRx, EMR, PQRS, Meaningful Use, MIPS, and MACRA.

These protocols were designed to improve efficiency and monitor quality, both reasonable goals when looking from the top down. However, if you switch places and look from the bottom up, that's when you spot the problem. By increasing the requirements for authorizations and referrals and imposing a "gatekeeper" on the system, you end up squeezing the physicians at the local level. Physicians then, in turn, had to hire more staff to handle all the new administrative tasks—an unreasonable amount of effort for many depending on the size of the practice—simply to comply with these regulations.

To most private practice physicians, these requirements were often first introduced as incentives but then became penalties if not adopted by a certain date. It was that "carrot-stick" method that resulted in an insidious alteration to the normal routine.

However, these nuisances obscure the larger, more profound issue at stake. In order to run a business successfully, you must have control over the prices you charge. You also must be able to establish your own internal business processes—protocols, standards, documentation, and systems. What does it matter whose name is on the door if that person is not in charge of how prices are set and how the office is run? The new system of managed care took authority away from doctors and gave it to third parties: government programs and insurance companies.

The die was cast—we now became, for all intents in purposes, employees of these large institutions. Yes, we owned our medical practices: our names were on the door, but THEY ran it.

In hindsight, what happened from that point on was inevitable.

The Medical System Becomes Tethered to Third Party Payors

Over time, the healthcare industry (for that is what it became, an industry) continued to undergo a transformation, further distorting the power dynamic between doctors and third-party payors (insurance companies, HMOs, and government programs). Wave after wave of corporate consolidation of insurance companies, hospital organizations, and healthcare management companies ended up creating mega institutions ruled by bottom-line economics. Like a game of Pac-Man, the individual players were devoured one by one, wiped from the scene. In the end, only a few of the individual players remained standing, still independent, still private.

Physicians became dependent upon these institutions, as well as government-sponsored programs, for the vast majority of their gross income, and this severely undermined their leverage. Consequently, third-party payors have been able to extract more and more financial concessions from doctors and place more and more requirements upon them—with what appears to be no end in sight.

Something happened within the healthcare ecosystem, something that feels like a bait-and-switch. What we doctors were expecting from our profession is not what we ended up with. While we devoted our full attention to the clinical aspects of delivering healthcare, the "business" of medicine grew and changed around us at a very rapid rate, as did power dynamics. One can hardly be faulted for having missed the bigger picture. We had patients to care for.

Here's the bottom line. Decisions regarding the delivery of healthcare used to be the domain of the professionals who **provided** the care–the DOCTORS. These decisions are now the domain of the entities **paying** for the care– the third-party payors.

With this shift toward the corporatization of healthcare, doctors have dropped a few notches in the chain of command. They are now considered "employees" within a larger system of insurance companies, hospitals, and government programs. Their wings have been severely clipped and their ability to make decisions about clinical care has been subordinated to the management tier above them.

One of the ways you see this happening is through language. Look closely and you will notice an insidious maneuver being carried out: the subtle but significant change in the words we use. Keep your eyes open for the strategic redefinition of terms. Ask yourself, when did the terms *doctor* and *physician* get replaced with the term *provider? Why did they do that?* How does that affect your relationship with the patient?

Physicians Are Not Providers!

Physicians did not go to provider school. They went to medical school, and they have medical degrees, not provider degrees. But notice how all that gets watered down by a small change in language. Dr. Dana Loñdono, urologist and founder of *Physician Coach Support* says this erosion of our title over time "is a powerful tool to confuse and dehumanize a physician. When you no longer know who you are, you will be lost."[16]

---

16   Londoño, Diana. "I'm a Physician, Not a Provider." KevinMD.com, July 21, 2022. https://www.kevinmd.com/2022/07/im-a-physician-not-a-provider.html.

It's not that hard to see now how patients began to conflate health insurance with healthcare. After all, doctors no longer have the final say over their patients' treatment. They are now outranked by bureaucrats, and they are no longer referred to by their hard-earned academic titles. Rather, they are lumped in with others under the ambiguous label of *provider*. But I am here to tell you...

Health Insurance Does Not Equal Healthcare!

Healthcare refers to the services doctors (after years and years of medical training) provide for their patients: examinations, diagnoses, and treatment plans. Health insurance is simply a risk management tool to protect an individual from catastrophic loss because of healthcare expenses. It is a tool to pay for healthcare; HOWEVER, IT IS NOT THE ONLY TOOL!

I'm not going to lie, it is challenging to explain the difference between healthcare and health insurance to some, especially when the common lexicon has these two terms meaning the same thing on the street. But it is critical that we draw attention to the difference. We must educate our patients and others in the healthcare ecosystem. I believe that this task will grow easier over time as people continue to question the need for health insurance coverage and reimbursement. It's not easy for people to admit it, but the light bulb usually doesn't go off in a patient's mind until his own health is on the line. And then, I've noticed, the patient wakes up pretty quickly.

Pros and Cons

Here's the tricky part: the third-party payor system does have its positives (when contained and limited), and at one time, the benefits of accepting third-party payment clearly outweighed the costs.

- It allowed doctors to outsource the intake of revenue and excuse themselves from the prickly discussions about payment. "You need to talk to your insurance company about an unpaid bill" is certainly a lot easier to say than "I need to talk to you about an unpaid bill."

- Insurance products also undoubtedly expanded the population of patients whom doctors could treat with the security of knowing that payment, for the most part, would be covered. No more wondering if a patient would run out on a bill.

- Participating in a provider network lessened or eliminated the work of building an initial patient base. Marketing, branding, and prospecting—the basic critical aspects of any business—are not an issue, as the system automatically sends a steady stream of patients through the doctor's door.

Obviously, these benefits still exist for doctors participating with third-party payors. Those are the "pros" of accepting insurance. Unfortunately, these benefits—as attractive as they may be—today can easily be outweighed by the costs and burdens of participating in the networks: the "cons." Some might even say that the benefits are barely perceivable anymore, given that they come at such a high cost. For example:

- The administrative requirements placed upon doctors are now overwhelming.

- Doctors have virtually no control over their practices' cash flow, at least not on the revenue side.

- The power wielded by the government and the insurance industry over doctors—including outright control of their practices—is slowly turning healthcare into a watered-down commodity, void of humanity and personalization of care. And it is turning patients and physicians into WIDGETS.

Our healthcare system was never intended or planned to operate this way. The problems we face today didn't occur overnight. They were the result of slow, gradual, systemic changes that eventually aggregated power in the hands of a small group of administrators and left doctors, the ones actually trained to provide medical care, in a position of impoverished authority and influence. It will take time, patience, discipline, and a concerted effort to regain physician independence and re-establish the physician-patient relationship as the foundation of medical practice.

CHAPTER 3

INFORMED CONSENT IS A TWO-WAY STREET

Let me remind you about something that you are very familiar with: *Informed Consent.* I know you know this concept because every medical student is drilled at great length on the importance of providing patients with *Informed Consent.*

In the doctor-patient relationship, there exists a power imbalance. The doctor has more information than the patient by nature of the doctor's education, experience, and possession of test results and other data. Before a patient can give consent to any medical treatment, the power imbalance must be rectified as much as possible. The doctor must do his or her best to make sure the patient understands:

- The complete nature and extent of the situation.

- The medical solution that is being recommended.

- The potential risks associated with the solution.

- The potential benefits.

- All possible alternatives to treatment.

Now take this concept and apply it to your own decision-making process regarding insurance contracts. Did anyone take you aside and make sure you had *Informed Consent* before you signed those papers? Did anyone make sure you understood:

- The complete nature and extent of the contract.

- The payment arrangement that was being offered.

- The downsides to that arrangement.

- The upsides to that arrangement

- Possible alternatives.

We all know the importance of supplying information to our patients before they give consent to treatment. But we were never taught the importance of informing ourselves before consenting to reimbursement arrangements with the insurance companies.

Doctors may have been naive there for a while; I'll admit that I was. I really thought I had done my due diligence. I even had a healthcare attorney review my agreements. On paper, the stipulations of the contracts appeared to be standard and straightforward—reimbursement rates, covered services, provider network, claims processing, quality metrics, length of contract, termination clause, and all the legal requirements for the state.

However, what was not spelled out (and why would it be when no one was asking?) were all the subtle ways in which the contracts gave the insurance companies significant leverage over me, just as they give the insurance companies significant leverage over all doctors:

- Doctors are led to believe they can negotiate reimbursement rates with an insurance company, but soon enough they realize it's a David versus Goliath scenario. (At least David knew what he was getting into. He volunteered for that fight.)

- Doctors want to think that patients are coming in to see them because they chose them. In actuality, there is no choice involved. It's all pre-selected. Patients go to see doctors because doctors are in their insurance provider's network, and they don't want to pay anything more than the predetermined amount. It's nothing personal. If a doctor isn't in the network, patients with that insurance will go somewhere else.

- Doctors have no control over cash flow in their practice. It doesn't matter if a doctor has already treated and discharged a patient. Insurance companies have complete control over claims processing, and they make no apologies for the length of time it takes to reimburse a doctor or for the penalties linked to denied claims.

- A doctor may think that their sound medical diagnosis and treatment protocol is sufficient to justify full reimbursement for a service. However, insurance companies may require her to meet certain quality metrics—such as patient satisfaction scores—before they reimburse her.

In more recent years, it has been these "quality metrics" that have added numerous administrative tasks for both the physician and office staff. These metrics fall into the following three broad categories:

- **Clinical Quality Measures**: clinical guidelines, patient satisfaction scores, treatment outcomes.

- **Utilization Measures**: frequency of visits, duration of visits, hospital admissions, frequency/types of tests ordered, frequency of procedures performed.

- **Cost Measures**: total amount spent on medical services per patient and per provider.

Failure to meet these and other metrics can result in reduced reimbursement or denial.

And what exactly does this do clinically for the patient who is sitting in front of you?

Does all of this really improve quality?

Doctors must learn to insist upon the same rights and protections for themselves that they provide their patients. Consent cannot be granted when there is an imbalance of information between the doctor and payor or, in other words, ***an imbalance of power***. This is not an ethical arrangement. And it will only change when doctors begin to demand *Informed Consent* for themselves.

CHAPTER 4

MENTAL CONDITIONING MATTERS

Have you ever wondered why it is so difficult for doctors to define the value of their services in monetary terms, while plumbers (and lawyers and electricians and accountants and so on) have no trouble looking a client in the eyes and presenting her with a bill and terms of payment? In this chapter, I will shed light on the internal struggle many doctors experience when they think about placing a dollar value on their services. Why does it create such a stumbling block? Here's a hint: mental conditioning.

A Mindset Forms One Thought at A Time

If you ask any doctor why he or she went into medicine, you are likely to get one or some combination of the following responses:

- *I liked science.*

- *I wanted a challenge.*

- *I wanted a noble profession that provided both job and financial security.*

However, the number one response to that question is this:

- *I went into medicine because I wanted to help people and make a difference in the lives of my patients.*

What about you? Who inspired you to become a physician? Was it your childhood pediatrician? Perhaps another doctor you met as a teenager or college student? Maybe it was a parent or another relative or even a fictional character.

Most doctors remember who first inspired their dream of wearing the "white coat" and being called "Doctor." You don't easily forget the person who filled you with high hopes and aspirations of success.

Then there are all the depictions of doctors in our culture. The brilliant doctor. The down-home country doctor. The hero doctor. The compassionate doctor. The funny doctor. In what ways did these depictions inspire your dream?

You find doctors everywhere in our media—from Norman Rockwell paintings in *The Saturday Evening Post* to *Peanuts* cartoons in the newspaper to television shows like *St. Elsewhere* and *ER* and *Chicago Hope*. Think of all the intriguing cases on *House* or the behind-the-scenes hijinks on *Grey's Anatomy* you watched when you were younger and full of idealism. This kind of cultural programming rooted us in a certain mindset, a sense of idealism, a belief in the way things ought to be, and a blindness to the political and economic realities in the world.

When you think back on the doctors who inspired you or the whimsical portrayals of doctors in the media, do you remember anyone ever having an in-depth discussion about the *price of care rendered*? Did Derek Shepherd on *Grey's Anatomy,* for example, ever go through an itemized medical bill line-by-line with a patient and explain the Byzantine insurance regulations? No? Why is that? Probably because such a conversation would not have made for good television entertainment. But what about Patrick Dempsey—the actor who played the doctor? My guess is he certainly went line-by-line through his payment contract. Or at least his agent did. Why? Because that made good business sense.

Youthful idealism isn't anything new, and it is nothing to be ashamed of. It fueled your desire to make a difference in the world. It motivated you to make the sacrifices necessary to get into medical school.

At some point, however, the daydream ended and the hard work of becoming a doctor began. You rolled up your sleeves, stuck your head in your books, and committed your days and nights to making the dream a reality. Unfortunately, you did all this without fully grasping the economic reality you would encounter as a practicing doctor. This is not your fault.

An Incomplete Education

So, what about your schooling, where you were trained to become a doctor? Did the topic of *the price of care rendered* come up in school?

The rigorous curriculum and years of academic medicine with its focus on clinical work (pre-med years, medical school, internship, residency—and for some a fellowship) trained us well to provide excellent clinical care. There's no question about that. When we were in school, it was our full-time job to learn how to take care of patients; and that's a good thing because there was a lot to learn!

The logistics of remuneration (aka "how we would get paid") could wait. Or so it seemed. We had enough on our plates. It was easier to assume everything would work itself out in the end than to start worrying about something so far down the road.

The path, if you recall, was regimented and pre-determined every step of the way. In college, you kept your eye on the upperclassmen, and you followed the class ahead of you. Then you did the same thing in medical school–starting with your didactic classes in those first years and continuing through your clinical rotations as you progressed. In residency, you moved from being the peon intern to the junior, senior, and, perhaps, chief resident. Then for some, it was off to do a fellowship.

So much hard work. So much to learn. And yet, the topic of *the price of care rendered* was likely never brought up in all that time. Shouldn't we have been prepared for the economics of our profession along with clinical training? As I alluded to earlier, we weren't in school to become monks–so why did the topic of remuneration never come up?

A Culture of Conformity

A scientific mind is a curious mind, a questioning mind. This seems like a rather obvious statement. Nothing controversial. After all, it was your scientific mind, your inquisitive mind, that propelled you into medical school in the first place.

At each stage of your training, you took advantage of every opportunity to learn–as a student, as a resident, and as a new physician. You observed. You examined. You took histories. You learned how to look for symptoms and use deductive reasoning. The *See One, Do One, Teach One* method became a way of life, a way of survival, a way of success. A tradition!

While this way of learning was, on one level, very effective, on another level it had some drawbacks—drawbacks that weren't readily apparent. As you were learning from those ahead of you how to care for patients, you were also learning (on an unspoken level) to do what you were told or shown—to comply with the instruction, not to question it.

The open exchange of inquiry and debate you likely engaged in as an undergraduate in a college classroom was not the modus operandi or standard behavior in medical school or residency. It wasn't that you didn't have an interchange of ideas, but the conversation in those spaces likely stayed within the bounds of a clinical case rather than ventured off into the realm of free and probing thought. Your focus remained day in and day out, on absorbing instruction. This wasn't the case just for you. This was the case for all of us. We all were subjected to this mental conditioning.

We all cut our teeth on the *See One, Do One, Teach One* method—effective in a practical sense, yes, without a doubt. We didn't have to wrestle with figuring out things on our own when there was a solid tradition supporting our decision-making. But at the same time, this approach, which was firmly entrenched in a hierarchical system, did have the effect of blunting intellectual curiosity.

Starting at the bottom of the hierarchy, we—as doctors-in-training—hesitated to question or go against tradition. Who were we to challenge anything we were being taught? Perhaps we feared retaliation if we did, or ostracism—being excluded from a cool case or from scrubbing in or doing a procedure or presenting a case. The competitive impulse is strong among us, and FOMO is real.

But then again, perhaps we adopted a compliant nature simply out of humble esteem for those with greater experience. There is much to be said for that. However, no matter how admirable deference for those ahead of us is, at some point blind compliance crosses over from respect to complacency and then to indoctrination. As Dr. Arlen Myers, otolaryngologist and president of the Society of Physician Entrepreneurs, says, physicians are "socialized to conform, not deviate."

Three, Two, One—Launch

Then came the day you graduated from training and began practicing. It is at this point that many doctors begin thinking for the first time about the financial consequences of the future, for this is when student loan repayments typically start coming due. Going forward, you had two choices: work for yourself in private practice or seek employment within a healthcare organization.

In my case, I opted for employment and joined a small medical group. It was a traditional insurance-based practice, and I was told that if I wanted to start working, I had to get on the insurance plans. This didn't raise any red flags for me, because it was the norm. Plus, it's what I had learned from my parents, both of them doctors who were still practicing at the time.

If you opted for employment with a hospital, you went through the same process; part of credentialing by the medical staff involves getting on the insurance plans. You probably didn't even question it. In fact, it was almost unheard of not to be on insurance.

Conforming to the *See One, Do One, Teach One* approach to advancement in medicine, you watched those ahead of you sign the insurance contracts. Then you signed the contracts. And then you showed those behind you how to sign the contracts. And so, the beat goes on. Do you see how easy it was to fall into this rhythm?

You were conditioned to conform during your training, and at the same time, you weren't told the whole story about third-party payors. It's no wonder you find yourself in your current predicament. It's only after you started hearing about, reading about, and seeing an alternative way of managing a practice that you even realized you've been stuck in a type of programming this whole time.

What I'm talking about here is a well-grooved thought pattern, developed over years of following the system, years of not rocking the boat, not lifting the curtain to peek at the gears in motion. This thought pattern always felt familiar to you, always felt comfortable. You became so accustomed to viewing things in a certain way, it never occurred to you to question your beliefs. Until now . . .

- Now that you've begun to understand the history of our system of payments.

- Now that you've begun to inform yourself and acquire new knowledge.

- Now that you've come to understand that *Informed Consent* must be a two-way street.

But don't let any of this get you down!

That was the past and this is now. And what's happening now is that you are contemplating taking steps to move forward—you are examining where you are in your career and thinking intentionally about where you want to be in the future. And if you haven't yet picked up on what I've been trying to say: you can change your circumstances. It's YOUR choice! That knowledge should empower you.

Shifting your mindset will have to be a conscious choice on your part. Keep in mind that, without that shift, there can be no real change. You can't fake it, but you also shouldn't force it either. It will come about slowly as you acquire knowledge, apply what you learn and begin practicing in a new way.

The point of shifting your mindset is to develop a new perspective. And the point of developing a new perspective is to regain control and autonomy over your private practice. Keep reminding yourself of this because THIS IS YOUR *WHY*!

Price of Care Rendered Revisited

So, with a fresh set of eyes, look again at the concept of *the price of care rendered*. It's not a dirty word or a taboo topic. It has always been part of the equation, even if no one bothered to explain it to us or to include us in the discussions behind the scenes.

It could be tempting to ask, *why was it never discussed? Was this by design? Were we intentionally kept in the dark?* Looking for answers to those kinds of questions is a trap you want to avoid. There is no need to contemplate conspiracy. Use your energy to change what is within your power to change—namely, how you run your practice.

Ok, so you have all this new information. And your perspective is beginning to shift. This probably feels both exciting and scary at the same time. Why scary? Well, there are probably a few nagging concerns lingering, and justifiably so, like *How exactly am I going to make this happen?* and *How will I set my prices and communicate them to my patients?*

This is all totally normal. You can have those questions in your head, and even more questions than that, and still give yourself credit for being several steps closer to your goal than you were when you first picked up this book.

As far as those nagging questions go, a quick reframing of the thoughts will help. Flip those questions and make them statements of belief: *I'm going to figure out how to do this!* and *I'm going to find out how to set prices and communicate them to my patients!* You can believe these statements because you can see that there are doctors who have already figured it all out. These are not far-fetched objectives. Let me be the proof you need.

Like I said earlier, when you boil it down, much of building your Direct Care practice amounts to nothing more than common sense logistics and mathematics, both of which I'll be covering in this book and both of which are easy enough for someone as highly educated as you to grasp. Beyond that, it will be a matter of problem-solving using a form of intellectual know-how you already possess. How do I know you already possess this? Because it is the same intellectual know-how you apply right now when managing your patients and their issues. Only now you'll be applying these skills to the management of your practice.

Of course, it will take time and effort. You didn't get to this point in your career overnight and things are not going to change overnight. You'll likely encounter setbacks and challenges along the way, but if you can cultivate and nurture a growth mindset—one that is open, curious, and willing to learn—you will be well on your way to recognizing a new way of thinking and a new perspective.

As we conclude Section One, you now have everything you need to see the bigger picture and the *who-what-when-why-how* that has been undergirding your old mindset. You might need some time to stop, study, and reorganize your thoughts and contemplate these individual pieces. At some point, however, you will need to decide (and yes, it is a decision you make, no one makes it for you) to put the old mindset aside and start building a new one, a Direct Care mindset. When you do, you'll begin to see that Direct Care is all about choices—choices for you and choices for your patients. And choice is good. Choice is power. Choice is freedom.

And so, if you've made the choice to shift your mindset and move on, well then . . .

LET'S GO!

SECTION 2

ANALYZING YOUR CURRENT PRACTICE

"Business is all about numbers, and your numbers are telling you a story. And if you want to be in business for the long haul, you need to understand that story."
- Steve Forbes, publishing executive and
editor-in-chief of *Forbes*

In Section One, you received a history lesson designed to help you understand the situation doctors find themselves in today. After reading the first four chapters, your eyes should be wide open to the dysfunction within the system. You should be able to see now how this dysfunction is negatively impacting not only physicians but also the consumers of healthcare services—*your patients*.

Next on the agenda is an examination of your practice and its financial health. By that, I mean a hard look at the data. I like to think of this as reviewing blood work and other diagnostic tests. In Section Two, I will help you identify and analyze the markers of your practice's financial health to empower your decision-making.

These numbers and ratios—known as Key Performance Indicators (KPIs)—can be found by measuring various forms of activity in your practice. After providing a general definition of KPIs, I'll explain how they can serve as clues to the financial performance of any business.

From there I will move on to discussing the specific KPIs used to analyze a medical practice. I will explain how to calculate each one and then how to use it to analyze your practice. Along the way, I will also take you on a wild ride through the Revenue Collection Cycle of your medical practice. This is the process by which your office converts payments due from patients, insurance companies, and other third-party payors into the cash your practice needs to meet its financial obligations. I realize there is a lot of information packed into Section Two, so I've done my best to break it down into easily digestible chunks.

As you absorb this new information and begin sizing up the KPIs of your own practice and Revenue Collection Cycle, don't allow yourself to get flustered by any one number or any one outcome. Taken alone, they are simply data points gathered from different angles. They provide insights from various perspectives. Each one offers a clue to your business's overall health—but only one clue. The more complete picture will arise from the comprehensive analysis of all the numbers. This will be explained as we go along.

For any of you who have doubts about your ability to learn this, I want to challenge you on two things: your intellectual ability and your professional responsibility. First, it's complete nonsense to think that you, with all that you've accomplished academically and professionally, don't possess the skills necessary to perform a business analysis. And, secondly, it's YOUR practice we are talking about, so ultimately the buck stops with you, the owner of the private practice. You need to be involved with the numbers. Think of it this way. Would you let a medical student or resident sign off on a chart? Of course not.

Not many people (if any at all) told us that a doctor can simultaneously treat patients AND manage the business end of a private practice. Furthermore, virtually no one told us it was our responsibility to do this. So now, when it comes to examining the numbers, you might find yourself fully under the spell of learned helplessness without even knowing it. Well, that stops here.

This is not to say that the business of healthcare isn't touched on, at least briefly, in some medical schools. But for many of you currently practicing medicine, it probably wasn't a part of the curriculum when you were in medical school. Fortunately, that seems to be changing, as many younger physicians now report having learned about healthcare financing, insurance systems, and regulatory laws.

If you were taught anything at all, you very likely were taught that health insurance is what controls the healthcare payment system; however, beyond that, you probably weren't told how it works or how it relates to a doctor's bottom line. *Out-of-sight / out-of-mind*. That's the basic mentality in residency. As long as our paychecks cleared, we simply assumed everything was running as it should, so we didn't feel compelled to investigate further.

But no more. It is time to grow beyond that mindset; it is time to overcome all hesitations. You know very well that you need to get into the numbers of your practice and start paying close attention. On the surface, this might seem like dry material, but once you start mastering and applying the concepts, the business side of your practice will no longer be a mystery.

At a fundamental level, the clinical work of a doctor boils down to the analysis of data—more specifically, the analysis of data collected from different perspectives. It's the same basic principle in business, just different terminology.

To successfully manage the business side of a medical practice, you need to be able to think on the fly, develop proper plans and then execute those plans. Stop and reflect on this for a moment. Do those skills sound familiar? They should because these are the skills you already possess and use daily as a doctor! This revelation should come as a relief.

From the moment you enter an exam room and see your patient, you instinctively begin the process of history-taking through observation and inquiry. This very same dynamic will play out as you examine your practice. Your relationship with the business end of your practice will develop and grow stronger the more intimately you know and understand the hard data.

What I am trying to say here is simple: entrepreneurship requires a certain skill set, and that skill set can be taught. Indeed, it is taught. There's a pedagogy for it, and many people commit themselves to learning it. Furthermore, they hand over good money to acquire it. But, as a practicing physician, YOU ALREADY POSSESS THIS SKILL SET. You now simply need to recognize that you have these skills and apply them in pursuit of a different objective: managing the business end of your practice.

CHAPTER 5

NUMBERS EQUAL POWER

Remember, as a physician owner, you are the CEO of a business—your private practice. That means the buck stops with you! Set aside your clinical responsibilities for a moment and **let's look at things strictly from a business perspective.** For your small business to survive—and more importantly for it to thrive—it is critical that you **know your numbers and monitor your key metrics**.

Numbers should not intimidate you, for numbers are nothing more than data. As a physician, you interpret data every day; therefore, reviewing the numbers of your practice should be no more challenging or intimidating than reviewing labs and diagnostic tests.

In business, strategic operating numbers and ratios are known as Key Performance Indicators or KPIs. If you take the time to master these metrics, they will become powerful tools at your disposal. They will allow you to gauge the financial health of your practice and spot opportunities for improvement.

In the next several chapters, I will define and explain the KPIs of a medical practice. I will show you how to calculate them and then how to use them as tools to analyze the financial performance of your practice and make strategic decisions to improve upon that performance. It's how I learned how to manage a successful Direct Care practice, and it's how you can too.

I like to tell my clients: *numbers equal power*. To illustrate that point, I break it down like this:

1. *If you don't know your numbers, you don't have data.*

2. *If you don't have data, you can't measure.*

3. *If you can't measure, you can't improve.*

4. *If you can't improve, you have no control.*

5. *If you have no control, you have no power.*

You are the one who should be in control of your practice, and no one else! So, you need to know your numbers.

Each type of business (from retail to hospitality to transportation and so on) has its own set of KPIs, and savvy business owners follow their KPIs religiously. They use them to measure business performance from different angles—volume, profitability, productivity, efficiency, etc. They use them to measure business performance over various periods: hourly, daily, weekly, monthly, quarterly, annually, etc.

Your KPIs will provide you with the means to track what is working well in your business and pinpoint what needs to be improved. And remember, when you can improve, you have control. And when you have control, you have power.

A medical practice, however, is a highly nuanced business and thus its KPIs are highly nuanced as well. Because this is so, I find it often helps my physician clients to grasp the intrinsic value of KPIs in general if they first take a look at the concept through the lens of a business everyone is familiar with as consumers. I typically use the restaurant business.

So, imagine that you own a restaurant. Then follow along as I point out the various performance indicators a restaurant owner can analyze and improve upon using the KPIs of a restaurant business. The goal of this exercise is to provide you with a framework for understanding the usefulness of KPIs in general, regardless of the type of business.

Despite the vast differences between running a medical practice and running a restaurant, both of these businesses are governed, in a broad sense, by basic business fundamentals. To help drive that point home, ask yourself the following questions as we examine situations in your restaurant:

- *What concerns and considerations do you and a restaurant owner have in common as business owners?*

- *What similar goals do you share?*

- *Do you notice how these goals can be pursued effectively using smart management tools like KPIs?*

So, here we go. Let's imagine you own a popular specialty sandwich bistro in town. To stay in business, your restaurant must generate enough Revenue to cover the Expenses of running the bistro. These are the first two metrics for you to take note of--Revenue and Expenses. Inflow must exceed outflow. This is a very rudimentary law of business.

Let's use these two metrics to analyze a few hypothetical scenarios in your bistro. Say you charge $20 (Revenue Metric) for a Reuben sandwich, and your restaurant is booked solid every day with people eating Reubens.

Lots and lots of Revenue. That sounds like a reason to celebrate, right? *Yay, the business is successful. It's bringing in lots of Revenue*. But wait, not so fast. What does it cost you to make that Reuben sandwich? By that, I mean what is the Cost of Goods Sold (Expense Metric)? If you have to spend $25 for labor and raw material to make and serve that Reuben sandwich, you are losing $5 on every sandwich you sell. So, selling more and more sandwiches, although it seems exciting, is costing you more and more money, which is not exciting. It is upside down. You might be popular and well-loved, but you won't be in business for very long.

What does this tell us? You can't look at Revenue in a vacuum; you must look at it in comparison to Expenses. Revenue that is too low is a problem. Sure, that's easy to understand. But so are Expenses that are too high relative to Revenue, especially if they exceed Revenue. It's important to notice that it's not just one number here or there that provides all the answers but rather it is the relationship between the numbers that is most revealing.

With the help of KPIs, you can make strategic management decisions to shift your business in the right direction. For example, in your hypothetical bistro, now that you know you are losing money on the Reubens, you can consider raising the price of that sandwich. Or, instead, you can look into sourcing the ingredients at a lower price. Or maybe you can do both. One thing is for certain: without KPIs, you can't make an informed decision. And without KPIs, you can't track the impact of those decisions you make.

But there's even more insight to be derived from your Revenue number. When you take Total Revenue and break it down by each service and product, you access a deeper level of insight. Total Revenue indicates how well your business is doing in general—on the whole. But when you break this gross number down by categories, you get to see which products and services are contributing the most to the top line.

It is important for you, the bistro owner, to know how much of your Total Revenue is coming from Reuben sandwiches. How much from ham sandwiches? How much from desserts? From drinks, etc. Let's say 50% of your Total Revenue is coming from Reuben sandwiches and 9% is coming from ham sandwiches. What does that tell you about consumer demand? How might this information be helpful when deciding how to allocate resources? You always want to be mindful of consumer preferences. It doesn't matter if you love ham sandwiches and wouldn't be caught dead eating a Reuben. What matters is what your consumers prefer.

Just a side note here that might help put Revenues and Expenses in perspective: when I think about Revenue and Expenses in my business, it's kind of like Ins & Outs charting we use to determine a patient's fluid volume. With a business, we measure Revenue (funds flowing into the business) and Expenses (funds flowing out of the business).

Now back to the bistro. Just as you can deconstruct the Revenue number, you can also deconstruct the Expense number to see what's going on, product by product or service by service. The Cost of Goods Sold (COGS) metric is fairly self-explanatory. It's the amount it costs you to provide your products and/or services to the consumer. COGS can be broken down by each service and by each product. When you subtract COGS from Revenue you get your Gross Profit number.

We've already seen that the Gross Profit on the Reuben sandwich is negative $5, meaning that for every Reuben you sell you are losing $5. Not good. Let's say the Gross Profit on the ham sandwich is positive $8. Who knows? Maybe corned beef for Reubens costs twice as much as ham costs for ham sandwiches. This information changes things quite a bit. It gives you more information to consider before you make any decisions. Your bistro sells more Reubens, but you are losing money on them. Your bistro sells fewer ham sandwiches, but ham sandwiches are making you a tidy profit. Hmm? Is the profit you make on selling ham sandwiches enough to offset the loss on the Reubens? Maybe? These are the kind of questions you will wrestle with once you get into the numbers behind the numbers.

Keep in mind that the KPIs don't tell you what to do with your business. Rather, they allow you to make informed decisions because they offer you perspectives from different angles. You can move in many different directions with your bistro given the insight you've gained from these KPIs. And that's infinitely better than tossing and turning all night wondering why your business's bottom line is rather puny when so many people love your Reuben sandwiches.

At this juncture, it should be pointed out that Revenue is not always received in the form of cold hard cash. Your bistro might accept credit card payments. If that's the case, then you will have to expend time and effort to collect your cash from the credit card company. And that process—depending upon how long it takes—can create a lag in funds. Have you ever wondered why some businesses offer discounts for customers who are willing to pay in cash? Cash today is more valuable than cash tomorrow or three weeks from now or (yikes) three months from now. A lag in funds from the point of sale is what creates a difference between the Revenue Metric (the sale recorded) and the Cash Flow Metric (the receipt of cash on the books). As we go forward, keep this distinction in the back of your mind. Both metrics are important, but they measure different aspects of your business–different perspectives. You'll see in a few chapters why it can be argued that Cash Flow is the more important metric to keep your eye on, at least in the short term.

Now, before I wrap up this little introduction to KPIs, let me give you an example of how you might use a Consumer Metric (in medical practices it is known as a Patient Metric) to spot potential trouble in your bistro business. Let's say that the number of people coming to your bistro begins to decline. This could be a red flag, especially if the decline continues over an extended time with no reversals. Perhaps there is something wrong with the atmosphere of your bistro. Or maybe the quality of service in your bistro is falling off. By tracking your KPIs, you'll be able to spot such issues early on and address them before they do too much damage to your business. Similarly, in your medical practice, monitoring Patient Metrics like Volume, Retention Rate, and Referral Rate will help you gauge the strength of your patient base. It will offer you insights into patient satisfaction and help you identify areas where you can improve.

I hope this little game of make-believe has softened you up to the idea of KPIs and primed your appetite for numbers. (Apologies for the pun; perhaps I am getting a little too much into the mode of the restaurant owner.) Over the next several chapters, I'll identify and define the various KPIs and financial ratios of a medical practice. I will show you how to use information hidden in the numbers to adjust pricing strategies, improve billing processes, and implement patient retention initiatives, among other tricks.

Before we move on, however, I want to emphasize the importance of making financial monitoring a regular practice. Financial monitoring is not a *one-and-done* deal. This is a way of life, a habit of health, like brushing your teeth. You must stay consistent, set realistic goals, and communicate your findings with your team. And never hesitate to seek assistance from financial advisors or consultants who specialize in medical practices.

Moving forward, you will see I have broken down into five categories the Metrics that you, as the owner of a private medical practice, need to understand and monitor:

- Revenue Metrics

- Expense (Cost) Metrics

- Cash Flow Metrics

- Patient Metrics

- Reimbursement (Insurance) Metrics

As I mentioned before, there is also a chapter on the Revenue Collection Cycle of a medical practice. Just as your hypothetical bistro will experience a lag between the point of sale and the receipt of funds if you accept credit card payments, your medical practice—if it participates with third-party payor plans—will experience a lag between patient visits and receipt of funds. The chapter on the Revenue Collection Cycle will explain how complicated this process has become for insurance-based medical practices and how it can cause problems for you if it's not managed properly.

In the final chapter of this section, I will pull all this information together and provide you with specific financial ratios you can use to gain an even better picture of your practice's financial health. Remember, numbers equal power, and the goal of this book is to empower you.

CHAPTER 6

REVENUE AND EXPENSE METRICS

The first two KPIs I'm going to discuss are Revenue and Expenses. It doesn't get more basic than that. These two terms are fairly self-explanatory. Revenue represents the amount of money a business generates from selling products and services. Expenses represent the amount of money the business has to pay to provide those products and services. As I mentioned in the previous chapter, Revenue and Expenses are somewhat akin to the Ins/Outs that doctors monitor in patients.

Taken as a whole, the Revenue and Expense numbers provide a certain level of insight, but, as a business owner, you need to monitor financial operations from multiple levels, not just from a bird's eye perspective. You need to look from as many angles as possible. So, in this chapter, I'm going to show you how to slice and dice aggregate Revenue and Expense numbers into more refined metrics and how to analyze these two aspects of your business (inflow and outflow) from different perspectives. I'll then point out the various kinds of valuable insight we can extract from this analysis.

Starting with Revenue, we will look at it from the following angles:

- Total Revenue

- Revenue-by-Service/Product

- Revenue-by-Provider

- Average Revenue-per-Patient -Visit

After that, we will look at Expenses from the following angles:

- Total Expenses

- Cost of Goods Sold (COGS)

- Staffing Costs

- Facility Costs

In case you are worried about having to calculate these numbers yourself, fear not. There are a variety of great management programs specifically designed for medical practices that can select the data and calculate these numbers as needed. What you need to focus on at the moment is learning what the metrics represent and how they can be used to make decisions.

Revenue Metrics

Total Revenue

Total Revenue equals the overall amount of services and products your medical practice sells during a particular period: daily, weekly, monthly, annually, etc. It's just like the total sales of a restaurant.

You calculate Total Revenue by adding up the amount charged for all services and products sold by your practice, regardless of the form of payment received, whether it is cash, insurance, or a payment plan. Revenue **does not always** equate with Cash Flow. **Don't forget this!**

Monitoring your Total Revenue provides you with a high-level view of your practice's top-line performance. Are overall sales going up, going down, or staying steady? This is the question you will be asking yourself when you check this KPI.

Revenue by Service/Product

As mentioned in the previous chapter, your Total Revenue number can be (and should be) broken down by each product and service your practice offers. It is important to know which products and services are contributing the most to Total Revenue and which ones are contributing the least.

Take each product and service you offer and total the revenue your practice earns from each one, or simply maintain a running total of each product and service at all times. Be sure to include anything and everything that generates revenue for your practice: consultations, procedures, diagnostic tests, in-office products, etc. Every last dime of Total Revenue should be accounted for when broken out by category.

After you tally each revenue category, you can then calculate each product and service's contribution as a percentage of Total Revenue. This will allow you to size up products and services in relative terms as well as absolute terms.

Let's say your Total Revenue is $100,000 and when you break open this number and look at the components you find out Procedure A generated $30,000, Procedure B generated $25,000, Procedure C generated $20,000, and in-office products generated $25,000. Your breakdown of Revenue-By-Service/Product would look like this:

Procedure A - $30,000 - 30% of Total Revenue

Procedure B - $25,000 - 25% of Total Revenue

Procedure C - 20,000 - 20% of Total Revenue

In-Office Products - $25,000 - 25% of Total Revenue

Maybe it never dawned on you how important in-office products were to your overall business. Maybe you were thinking of scaling them back to create more seating in your waiting room. But now, armed with this breakdown of Total Revenue, you can see exactly how that decision might impact your top line.

Revenue by Provider

(Please note, I do not like to refer to physicians as "Providers," because I feel this term is being used disrespectfully these days to devalue physicians within corporatized healthcare systems. This will be the only time I refer to physicians as "Providers" in this book.)

The Revenue by Provider metric offers you another perspective on Total Revenue. It allows you to track revenue contributions by each revenue producer in your practice (be they a physician, nurse, or other specialist on your staff).

To calculate this metric, take each revenue producer in your practice and add up the amount each one contributes to Total Revenue. In a group practice, multiple physicians contribute to the practice's Total Revenue. But keep in mind if you are in a solo practice your assistants, when utilized efficiently, can function as physician extenders and, under your supervision, can be revenue producers too, generating their revenue stream.

Monitoring Revenue by Provider allows you to assess the absolute contribution of each provider to Total Revenue as well as the relative contribution. It helps you identify high-performing providers and those who may need additional support. By analyzing this data properly, you can optimize scheduling, incentivize top performers, and/ or address performance gaps.

Average Revenue Per Patient Visit

This metric reveals how much revenue each patient visit generates on average. If a restaurant owner knows how much each customer spends on average, he can quickly get an idea of how much his restaurant is taking in at any given moment (or over any period of time) simply by totaling the number of customers and multiplying by the average revenue per customer number. You can make the same rough calculation if you know your Average Revenue Per Patient Visit metric.

To calculate Average Revenue Per Patient Visit, divide your Total Revenue for a certain period of time by the total number of patient visits during that time period. This will give you a bird's-eye view of your overall practice; however, you can always tighten your focus and obtain greater insight by calculating this number for each specific revenue producer.

One Doctor's Story - Revenue Diversification

We all remember how clinics shut down and surgery schedules were interrupted during the pandemic. This, as you well know, created financial stress for many physicians, especially surgeons. It was a time when the financial vulnerability of medical practices became evident to many. Feeling squeezed by this situation, a colo-rectal surgeon came to me seeking advice. I helped him see that he could reduce his practice's financial dependence on his caseload if he diversified his revenue stream.

We talked about the type of patients he was treating, their issues, and their recovery rates. He lamented the fact that generally speaking, he was seeing patients who should have come to him earlier. His patients should have had an earlier screening, he said. If they had, he could have done more for them. For the most part, his patients were coming to him as referrals from primary care doctors and gastroenterologists in the community.

"Why wait for referrals?" I asked him. "You could offer the screenings yourself and create a new revenue stream for your practice." He had never thought of that but liked the idea. We began working on a strategy for incorporating screening consultations into his practice.

I checked in with this doctor a year later and learned that the new strategy was paying off on many levels. After he implemented expanded screening services in his practice, many primary care physicians and gastroenterologists began referring patients to him for screenings. By doing so, these doctors were able to ease their office load and remove one step in the referral process. The community was responding enthusiastically to the availability of more avenues for preventative care.

One year after this doctor and I discussed his desire to diversify his revenue stream, his patient visits had increased so much that he had to dedicate an additional day to seeing patients in the office. This meant less time in the OR. As a bonus, this additional day dedicated to the office gave him the flexibility to schedule some free time for himself when he wanted.

In the end, this one decision had a positive impact both on his practice financially, and personally for his well-being, and clinically on the overall preventative health of his community. This doctor would not have thought about expanding his practice in this way had he not been monitoring his revenue metrics.

Expense (Cost) Metrics

Total Expenses

Total Expenses is another aggregate number. It comprises ALL the operating expenses of your business: Cost of Goods Sold, Staffing Costs, Facility Costs, etc. Of course, it is important to be aware of what it costs to run your business overall, but there's not much you can do to reduce Total Expenses until you break this number down into its components.

Cost of Goods Sold (COGS)

Remember our discussion of COGS in the last chapter? The COGS for the Reuben sandwich included the cost of all the ingredients—the rye bread, corned beef, sauerkraut, Swiss cheese, etc.

In your medical practice, COGS represents the direct cost of providing medical services and products. For most offices, COGS will simply be the cost of medical supplies and pharmaceuticals used and consumed during patient visits. In some practices, however, COGS may also include the cost of using equipment, reagents, or machine-specific supplies to perform the service such as x-rays, lasers, ultrasounds, etc. Other offices might dispense in-office products such as medications or medical equipment, and in those cases, COGS will include the cost of acquiring the items dispensed.

Note that the calculation of COGS differs from practice to practice and will vary based on the types of services offered and the products provided. Don't get too hung up right now on the exact components of your COGS. What is important at the moment is for you to familiarize yourself with this term and understand how this metric can help you set goals to improve the financial performance of your practice.

You need to keep a close eye on the COGS of your practice. An increase in COGS represents a decrease in your gross profit. If your COGS starts trending upward, you will want to catch it early and consider new sources for your materials and supplies.

One Doctor's Story - Managing Expenses

For doctors who perform in-office procedures, sterilization of instruments is a daily requirement. It also represents an expense. Autoclaves cost money to operate and maintain and you also have to pay a staff member to perform the tasks. These are COGS.

One dermatologist I worked with as a client was frustrated because she was down to one autoclave (her other one had died) and the cost of using it and maintaining it was steadily increasing. Furthermore, one of her staff members was always tied up–for the whole day–cleaning and sterilizing instruments.

I talked to her about using pre-sterilized/disposable instrument packs. The peel-packs might be more convenient and cost-effective. Using the peel-pack instruments would reduce her practice's need for daily autoclaving operations, staffing, and maintenance.

The doctor canvassed different vendors to compare prices. As she looked at the options, I instructed her to weigh them against the cost of using the machine. I told her to consider everything: how often she ran the machine (weekly, monthly, etc.), the cost of maintenance, and how she would use the staffer who no longer had to clean and sterilize the instruments.

By doing a proper expense analysis, this dermatologist was able to make an informed decision about her COGS. She ultimately decided to transition to the peel-packs. This decision led to a reduction in overall expenses and thus an increase in the overall profitability of the practice. She no longer had to pay for operating and maintaining an autoclave. And the staff member was freed up to do other tasks in the office, improving overall efficiency.

Staffing Costs

Just like a restaurant needs a skilled and dedicated team to operate smoothly, your medical practice relies on its team of staff members to provide quality care. Staffing costs include salaries, wages, benefits, and other expenses associated with your employees (training, licensure, uniforms, etc.). It's important to track Staffing Costs to keep them in line with your budget and Total Revenue.

When teaching my physician clients about expense metrics, I recommend keeping Staffing Costs separate from COGS even when a staffer such as a sonographer or a phlebotomist performs a single, specialized service. In offices that follow best practices, staff members often cross-train for various roles. Therefore, I feel Staffing Costs should not be included in COGS.

By monitoring Staffing Costs, you will be able to assess productivity levels and identify opportunities to improve efficiency. In short, you will be able to make informed decisions about staffing levels.

Facility Costs

Your medical practice is likely conducted in a physical office, or facility, just like a restaurant has its own space. Maybe you own your space and pay a monthly mortgage. On the other hand, if you lease your space, then you pay rent.

Facility Costs include expenses associated with your physical place of business such as rent or mortgage payments, utilities, maintenance, and insurance. Maybe you don't see patients in a specific physical location of your own, but rather you see them in their homes. In that case, your Facility Costs will include your car, gas, and vehicle maintenance expenses. For telemed practices, Facility

Costs will include your internet connection, phone service, website hosting service, and any apps you use to connect with your patients or "see" them virtually.

Facility Costs are typically fixed costs, meaning they remain the same from month to month under a contractual agreement. Rent is usually the same from month to month. So is your insurance premium and your cleaning service and your lawn care. Utility expenses can vary but usually stay within a fairly consistent range.

It is important to be familiar with all the expenses that make up your Facility Costs. Monitoring Facility Costs, however, won't be as important in the short run, because they, for the most part, are fixed. On the other hand, when making long-range decisions, it's vitally important that you consider all Facility Costs and not underestimate your obligations in this category.

This now brings me to the end of my discussion of the Revenue and Expense Metrics of a medical practice. Are you starting to draw connections between the revenue and expenses in your practice? We covered quite a few terms, but I hope, after reading through these last few pages, you see how rather simple these metrics are to calculate. And how much value they offer you when it comes to making strategic decisions about your practice.

Most of the work so far has involved little more than taking big fat numbers and breaking them down into component parts to gain a more intimate understanding of your practice and its workings. Just as your relationship with a patient grows through an understanding of that patient's numbers, so will your relationship with your practice grow as you begin to understand its numbers. But this takes time. And you've only just begun this journey. So don't be hard on yourself and don't feel rushed.

CHAPTER 7
REVENUE COLLECTION CYCLE

Fair warning: This is a longer and more detailed chapter for a reason. In my experience, many physicians have never been walked through the intricacies of converting their practice's revenue to cash and, as a result, many of them assume this process functions on autopilot. The same goes for patients. However, I'll let you know, it's been my experience that once clients are presented with the opportunity to intimately examine their collection cycles up close and in detail, things become very clear to them. Their eyes open. They start to understand what's going on. And they begin to see where things can be turned around! So, I urge you to spend time with this chapter learning the steps, reviewing the concepts, and then reference this material again later as needed.

It's time to talk about your practice's Revenue Collection Cycle. In case you aren't familiar with this term, it is the process by which your practice collects payment for your services.

There are two aspects of the cycle to take into consideration: (1) the individual steps that make up the Revenue Collection Cycle and (2) the length of time it takes to complete each one of those steps. **The more steps involved**, the longer it takes you to convert Revenue to Cash. And **the more time it takes to complete each step**, the longer it takes to convert Revenue to Cash. Those are the two factors to focus on: the number of steps involved and the length of time each step takes.

Revenue is said to be the lifeblood of your practice; although, if we look closer, it's really Cash Flow that keeps your business alive and kicking. Revenue represents the amount you've earned, not the amount you've actually received. You can earn an impressive amount of Revenue, but until it's realized in the form of cash, it cannot serve the needs of your practice. It's important to track both metrics: Revenue and Cash Flow. But it's also important to know which aspects of your business each metric measures and not to confuse the two.

In this chapter, I'm going to explain how the Revenue you earn is collected by your office and becomes cash in your bank account. The process plays out in a cycle. Revenue is earned when you provide a service or sell a product. This transaction kicks off the Revenue Collection Cycle process. At the end of the cycle, cash is received and becomes available to be used to meet the financial obligations of your practice.

Understanding and properly managing the Revenue Collection Cycle is critical for the financial success of a medical practice—of any business, for that matter. The cycle happens to be extraordinarily complicated for insurance-based medical practices. You'll see what I mean in a minute. However, before we get into the intricacies of a medical office's Revenue Collections Cycle, let me first present a very simple example of a Revenue Collection Cycle from a different type of business: a hotel. We've all stayed in hotels, so you should be able to relate to the following example.

The Revenue Collection Cycle of a hotel starts when you make a reservation. A credit card number is taken to reserve the room. You arrive at the hotel, check in, and then the hotel provides services (i.e., lodging, room service, etc.). At the end of your stay, you receive your bill with the services delineated. That white slip of paper silently appears under the door of your room on the day of checkout. And you pay for it. The bill is settled in full after your stay. If you pay by credit card, the hotel then processes that payment, and funds are transferred from the credit card company to the hotel, presumably several days later. And that concludes the hotel's Revenue Collection Cycle for your stay.

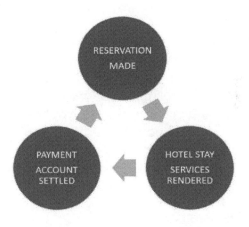

Figure 1. Revenue collection cycle for hotel

Now, let's look at a medical practice. The Revenue Collection Cycle begins when a patient contacts the office and schedules an appointment. The cycle ends when the practice gets paid *in full* for services rendered. Depending on the efficiency and the integrity of the individual steps of the process, the cycle can either sustain and energize your practice or it can create a great deal of distress for all parties involved–physician, staff, and patients!

By the way, each and every patient visit initiates a new and distinct Revenue Collection Cycle in a medical practice; therefore, on any given day, if you see more than one patient, multiple Revenue Collection Cycles will be launched in your system.

By accepting insurance as a form of payment from your patient, you are **providing your services in exchange for the right to claim payment** from the patient's insurance company, not from the patient (except for deductibles and copays). This is why it's called a third-party payor. You are the first party in the transaction. Your patient is the second party. And the insurance company or government program is the third party.

And this is why the Revenue Collection Cycle in an insurance-based medical practice can be so complicated. The person receiving your service walks away from the transaction with no obligation to make sure you receive your payment. And the third-party payor has incentives to delay (or even deny) your payment. Do you see the disconnect here? But I'm getting ahead of myself. First, let me break down the FIVE key components of the Revenue Collection Cycle of an insurance-based medical practice:

1. *Patient Registration*

2. *Appointment Scheduling*

3. *Patient Encounter*

4. *Billing & Invoicing*

5. *Payment Collection*

As I stated earlier, the various steps that make up the Revenue Collection Cycle can get very complicated and, when they do, the financial management of your practice can easily become muddled and unwieldy. You can "earn" Revenue by sharing your time, skills, and talents with a patient and you can be deserving of compensation for doing so, but, due to some breakdown here or there in the Revenue Collection Cycle, you might never receive compensation at all.

And this is why it is becoming more and more untenable to maintain an insurance-based practice. When you enter into a good-faith exchange of your time, skills, and talents only to realize that many third-party payors are not operating in the same good-faith manner but instead are ducking and hiding from their obligation to you—that's when you need to educate yourself on the games that are being played.

To help you grasp the importance of a healthy Revenue Collection Cycle, I'd like to draw a few parallels with something you are intimately familiar with—the digestion of your food. Just as your practice requires a healthy Revenue Collection Cycle to thrive, your body requires a healthy digestive cycle to function at its best. When you consume food, you expect it to nourish your body and provide you with sufficient energy to fuel optimal health. Some foods do indeed get digested properly and go on to contribute perfectly to the functioning of your body and its well-being. Some foods don't. And some foods, during the digestion process, actually cause problems for you.

Think about it for a minute: digestion is a complex process. It involves a series of functions, coordinated across various organs. Myriad biological processes must take place in proper sequence for food to be converted to energy in your body. However, as a doctor, you know that there are quite a few ways in which things can easily go wrong. Food can enter the body, but that food doesn't always digest properly and contribute positively to your health. And when your food isn't digested well, problems can arise, thereby opening the door to progressive dysfunction in the body.

Similarly, your practice's Revenue Collection Cycle can also malfunction. Revenue can be earned but not collected. As with your digestive cycle, there are quite a few ways in which things can go wrong in your Revenue Collection Cycle. You need to be aware of this and know that without healthy, efficient, and high-functioning cycles, (remember, each patient visit generates its own Revenue Collection Cycle) your practice can very quickly run into liquidity problems. Thus, you **MUST** keep your eye on the Revenue Collection Cycle process in your practice and familiarize yourself with how there might be a backup that could compromise your practice's financial health and viability, both in the short run and the long run.

Remember, it must run like a well-oiled machine!

As I've established, the Revenue Collection Cycle of an insurance-based medical practice involves multiple interactions and several variables. The greater the number of interactions and the greater the number of variables—the greater the potential for problems. Each patient generates his or her own unique Revenue Collection Cycle. Each cycle plays out through a series of interactions with each patient's insurance plan, governed by that plan's protocols, rules, and regulations, all of which must be navigated by the doctor's medical billing staff.

Most patients don't know the maneuvers that take place behind the scenes after an appointment is made, and sadly, many physicians don't either. So, let's break things down and look at each of the steps that make up your practice's Revenue Collection Cycle.

Patient Registration

When a patient contacts your practice for the first time, your staff begins the intake process by gathering the patient's demographics—name, date of birth, address, phone number, email, etc. This information is used to create a patient profile. However, in insurance-based practices, there is one more step beyond that: taking down the patient's insurance information. This insurance information is then used by your staff to determine if your office has a relationship with the patient's plan and, if so, if your office is considered *in-network* with the plan or *out-of-network*. Once that is settled, your staff will establish the type and amount of coverage the patient has under the plan.

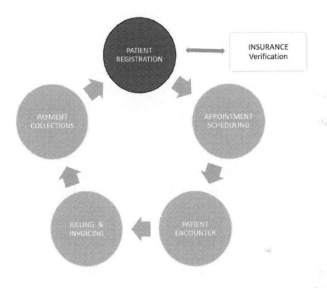

Figure 2. In an insurance-based practice, an additional network verification occurs during the patient registration.

Appointment Scheduling

Some offices will schedule a patient's appointment as soon as that patient completes the registration process– that is, as soon as the individual provides all the information requested. Many offices, however, won't schedule a patient until that patient's insurance has been verified and coverage determined. This can take time to accomplish. It varies from one insurance company to the next and from one plan to the next. This is just one of the many variables that have an impact on the quality of the cycle.

Patient Encounter

We include the patient encounter in the Revenue Collection Cycle because this is when you render your **services**. This is when you examine, diagnose and treat the patient. It is also the point at which additional **services** can be provided.

I've highlighted the word **services** twice to make a point that many of my physician clients often overlook: it's not just your time and service that you are giving to your patient during the patient encounter; it's the time you spent gaining the expertise, learning how to provide that service and the value of that time.

I say all this as a reminder to you to never forget the value of your knowledge and skills. And the value of the time you spent acquiring your knowledge and skills.

The patient encounter begins the moment your patient appears before you and the process of observation begins. Your mind goes to work taking note of the patient's appearance, demeanor, alertness, lethargy, etc. This is what your brain has been trained to do. It's part of the service you are providing. From observation, you move to interaction. You sit with your patient face-to-face, talking, asking questions, listening to the answers, and examining the patient. This, too, is part of the service you are providing. All of these actions that you take should be accounted for when you consider the value of your services. The services that come after that—labs, x-rays, and in-office procedures—are considered additional services. You perform these services in addition to the assessment and examination.

After the patient encounter, the patient's clinical notes typically get recorded in an Electronic Medical Record (EMR). Most offices have some type of method for tallying the services that have been rendered. For example, if a new patient comes into an office and is diagnosed with a fracture, a typical accounting for the services rendered would include the patient visit, radiographs, and a fracture boot. Each service provided during the patient visit gets tallied up into one itemized bill.

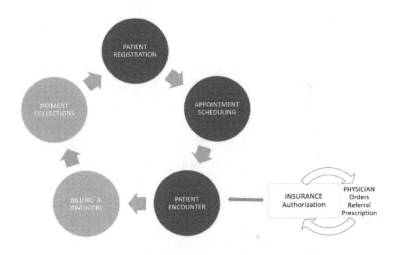

Figure 3. In an insurance-based practice, additional authorizations may need to be obtained following the patient encounter; however, resolution of this process does not contribute to the revenue collection cycle of the practice.

Something to note at this step in the Revenue Collection Cycle that is not part of it, but involves an extra action, is getting authorization for clinical orders, referrals, or prescriptions from the insurance company. Keep in mind that you are often the one who will have to get this, for the patient to receive the clinical treatment that you have deemed necessary. Yet, your office will not receive any revenue for this work – another physician, a facility, a lab or a pharmacy will. It makes you ask the question: *Why are you paying someone to do work for another entity to be reimbursed?* It makes you question: *Who is practicing medicine at this point?* When you order, refer, or write a prescription, *why is someone else giving you the OK to proceed?*

Billing & Invoicing

In cases where insurance is not getting billed for the services provided, the invoice will be presented directly to the patient for payment.

However, in an insurance-based practice, billing and invoicing are presented to an insurance carrier in the form of a claim. Each of the services rendered during the patient encounter is linked to a code called a Current Procedural Terminology (CPT) code. In the example above, there would be corresponding CPT codes for each of the services: (1) the physician's evaluation and treatment during the patient visit, (2) the radiographs taken based on the number of views and per side, and (3) the fracture boot that was dispensed.

In an insurance-based practice, your office must complete two steps at this point of the Revenue Collection Cycle that Direct Care practices do not; you have to submit the claim to insurance (Claims Submission) and then you have to go through the claims adjudication process (Claims Adjudication). So, pull back just a minute and remind yourself of the bigger picture. At this point in the Revenue Collection Cycle, you have provided your services. Your patient has received the benefit of your services. Payment to you for those services, however, will now remain in a state of limbo until the insurance process plays out. And this process—depending upon variables out of your control—could potentially become a drag on your Revenue Collection Cycle.

Claims Submission

Before we move further with our discussion, I need to define a couple of terms—a superbill and an insurance claim. A **superbill** gets generated after a patient encounter. It is generated from the EMR and includes the following:

- All the patient demographics.

- The insurance information.

- The International Classification of Diagnosis (ICD) codes are assigned by the physician.

- The appropriate CPT codes are linked to the services provided.

The **insurance claim** then gets created from the information included in the superbill. It is the insurance claim, not the superbill, which gets submitted to an insurance carrier for processing. The format of the claim is oftentimes referred to as the "HCFA / CMS 1500" (a government form created by the Health Care Financing Administration/Center for Medicare & Medicaid Services). The HCFA / CMS 1500 can be completed either electronically or on paper. It's up to you and the preferences of your staff.

Your office can either do its own billing, and by that, I mean to convert the superbill into a claim and send it directly to the appropriate insurance company, OR you can contract with a billing company to do this work for you. Mind you, this superbill/claims submission process plays out for every patient visit.

Claims Adjudication

Once a claim is sent to the insurance company, the processing (or adjudication) of that claim begins. Each third-party payor has its unique way of adjudicating claims (with its own set of requirements) according to the contract agreement.

During the process of adjudication, the insurance company reviews the codes you submitted and cross-references them with a designated fee schedule. It is this fee schedule that dictates the allowable payment for procedures.

The insurance company then cross-references the patient's contract with the claim you submitted to determine if the deductible has been met. It also, at this point, determines whether or not the patient has a copay responsibility. Additionally, once adjudicated, any further co-insurance and/or patient responsibility is then determined. The calculations are reported to your office in the form of an Explanation of Benefits (EOB) report, which breaks down payments and/or non-payments.

After the steps are completed, payment may be issued by the insurance company to the physician (if the appropriate checkbox on the 1500 indicates "accept assignment"), to the patient, or to a secondary insurance carrier (if that is indicated on the 1500).

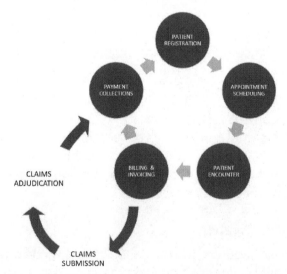

Figure 4. In an insurance-based practice, claims submission and adjudication occur prior to payment collection.

Payment Collection

Payment collection is the point in the Revenue Collection Cycle when your practice receives a cash payment for your services. If things were as simple as they are in the hotel business, payment would be collected in full at one single point in time. But this, unfortunately, is not how it works in an insurance-based medical practice. Instead, payment of your bill gets collected in various amounts and at different points in time. Why? Because part of it is paid by the patient and part is paid by the insurance company. Payment can come from the patient in the form of a **deductible responsibility**, a **co-payment**, or **co-insurance**. And payment comes from an insurance carrier in the form of a **reimbursement**.

- **Deductible**: the amount of medical expenses a patient must first pay out of their pocket before his insurance plan will pay anything towards a medical claim.

- **Co-payment**: a fixed payment for covered services as defined by a patient's insurance plan.

- **Co-insurance**: a patient's partial financial responsibility (as determined by the insurance plan) for covered services. Co-insurance is generally applied to a claim only after the patient has met his deductible.

- **Reimbursement**: a contractual payment by an insurance company towards the medical claim per specified CPT codes and their corresponding contracted fee schedule and payment protocol.

Your practice should receive correspondence from the insurance company with an appropriate EOB. The EOB should delineate what has been paid already (presumably by the patient), what remains to be paid, and who is responsible for the remaining balance due.

So, there you have it: a basic explanation of the five key components of a patient-initiated Revenue Collection Cycle in an insurance-based medical practice. As a reminder, those five steps are: 1) Patient Registration, 2), Appointment Scheduling, 3) Patient Encounter, 4) Billing & Invoicing, and 5) Payment Collection.

If all goes well, the Revenue Collection Cycle *should* conclude with full payment to your practice for the services rendered. But things don't always go well. You could render your services, file a claim for payment of those services, and then, lo and behold, end up with no compensation for your time, expertise, and knowledge. If a traveler skips out on his hotel bill, this is known as fraud. What is it called when a doctor's bill goes unpaid? And why is a doctor expected to be okay with this? Why is a doctor shamed for speaking up about this and attacked as being self-interested?

I should point out that when this happens, you might be able to seek recourse by refiling the claim or by appealing the denial. But then again, you might have no recourse at all. I'll explain.

The Potential for Roadblocks Is Great

Call them what you will—roadblocks, obstacles, hiccups, snags, stumbling blocks, jams—the number of ways in which an insurance company can interfere with your ability to get paid is too numerous to list in this one book.

However, let me go over some of the more common reasons insurance companies provide for denying a claim:

- *The service was not covered.*

- *Prior authorization was required.*

- *Patient information was incorrect.*

- *The service provided was not medically necessary.*

- *The claim was not filed within the allowable time limit.*

- *The patient's benefits could not be coordinated.*

To be clear, there are more reasons than these and there are variations on these six as well, but, for now, let's go through the ones I listed, for they are the ones you will see the most.

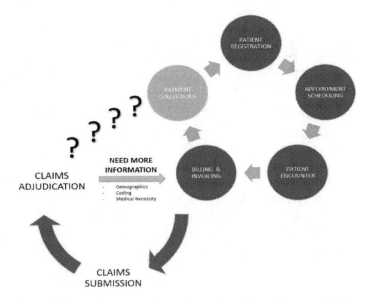

Figure 5. In an insurance-based practice, the outcome of claims adjudication is controlled by the third-party payor.

Service Not Covered

This is when you perform a service and then, after the fact, find out that the service is not covered under the patient's insurance plan.

When one of my claims is denied for this reason, it's typically related to a service I performed that (1) did not need prior authorization, (2) was a fairly routine service, and (3) was otherwise covered by the majority of insurance carriers. So, it can be confusing. You end up feeling left in the dark with this form of claim denial. So many questions come to mind. *Was the claim denied due to a contractual issue (something specifically excluded from the patient's plan)? Or was it an issue with the carrier's medical committee? Did they deem the service not medically necessary?* In which case, that's a separate issue.

I shared an example of this situation with you in a previous chapter—the patient with ingrown toenails on bilateral feet. I have always believed, in such cases, both toenails should be treated in one visit, so that's how I have treated those patients. Then, come to find out, some insurance carriers would reimburse for only one procedure and deny payment for the other. I would be informed, after the fact, that these patients should have been made to come in for two separate visits, one for each foot, for me to be paid for both procedures.

How, may I ask, are doctors and their office staff supposed to know such things in advance?

Prior Authorization Required

Some insurance plans require a patient to obtain pre-authorization for certain services. Failure to do so will result in a denial of reimbursement.

This is when an insurance company's protocol can interfere with a doctor's clinical decision-making. The doctor can be put in a difficult position, having to weigh the two choices, having to decide whether or not to perform the procedure—knowing that the procedure needs to be completed but also knowing that preauthorization for the procedure is required to be reimbursed. How is the doctor supposed to explain this situation to the patient? Should the doctor ask the patient to choose between his wallet and his health?

Believe it or not, it can get even worse than that. Let's say you get prior authorization and then go forward with the procedure, feeling you're doing the right thing for the patient and yourself, as well. You then submit the claim, fully confident you've followed the proper protocol. But the claim comes back denied. Some sort of glitch or snag. YES, this happens. Oftentimes it is a matter of *the left hand not knowing what the right hand is doing*. This is a fairly common occurrence within the bureaucracy of an insurance company. You may very well have obtained prior authorization, but if that information doesn't get relayed from one department to another within the insurance company, you will get a denial and the problem will be bounced back to you and your staff to figure it out.

Incorrect Patient Information

The devil is in the details, they say. There is so much room for error when taking down and inputting a patient's demographic or insurance information: missing name, wrong or misspelled name, wrong date of birth, incorrectly entered social security number, incorrectly entered insurance number, wrong address, omission of referring physician, and so on.

It was not that long ago that claims were submitted on paper. More recently, however, electronic submission has become the norm. This means quality control in your office is critical. You must make sure that every piece of information gathered and entered into the practice management software is 100% correct. Otherwise, your claim will be considered inaccurate and can be denied on that basis.

Despite receiving the claims electronically these days, many insurance companies still adjudicate the claims manually on their end. Oh, the irony! So, the risk of human error concerning data entry remains even if you've done everything correctly on your end. Oddly enough, when a human error at the insurance company does occur during manual entry, it's somehow not their problem. It's your problem. The doctor's office gets slapped with a denial and then must do the work of rectifying the mistake. Seriously?

Service Not Medically Necessary

If an EOB indicates that the service was not medically necessary, it's possible it merely requires additional information to adjudicate. This can entail requests for your medical records, a phone discussion with their medical officer, or proof of prior authorization.

If you are lucky, the insurance company will provide your office with a specific reason why the service was deemed not medically necessary. Even so, these determinations still baffle me. I am the one who examined the patient, not the insurance company. Shouldn't it be the doctor who sets the criteria for making that decision, not a bureaucrat behind a desk?

I recall times when the insurance company requested additional records to make a decision and I sent the records (along with an appropriate and logical justification supporting the need for the procedure), and yet the insurance company still deemed the request not medically necessary. You have to ask yourself, how are they coming to these conclusions?

This scenario can get out of hand quickly. Say the doctor is faced with a flat denial and no explanation for that denial; this results in a delay in reimbursement for the time being, followed by the initiation of the appeals process which can turn into something I call *appeals hell*. You can go through the entire appeals process and never really be told why the procedure was not medically necessary.

First, they will deny the claim and say the service was not medically necessary. So, you take some time, prepare your evidence to the contrary and submit it. What do you get back? A form letter stating, "The service has been determined to be not medically necessary." Seriously? Did they look at the information I submitted in the appeal? Or did they have the form ready to mail regardless of what I sent them on behalf of my patient?

Don't they realize I already know that they deemed the procedure not medically necessary? What I want to know is WHY!

What is worse is when you check on your appeal only to be told, "We have no record of any appeal." Again, why? Within the bureaucracy of these giant organizations, the departments aren't communicating with each other.

Timely Filing Limit

Claims must be submitted within a certain timeframe. Failure to do so can result in denials. Which seems reasonable.

However, what isn't reasonable is when an insurance company gets "creative" and redefines the timeframe, like changing the rules of a game while the ball is in play. Or they prolong the processing of the claim so long that the claim *times out*–but not because of any failure on your part. Or do insurance companies simply feel safe knowing there is not much doctors can do about it?

Back when I was still participating with insurance plans, my office typically filed our claims within one day of the date of service. In one instance, we submitted one claim on time, but it didn't get adjudicated for nine months, at which point it was denied. During the appeal of that claim, the one-year anniversary of the service date came up. The carrier looked at the date and denied the claim based on it not having been filed in a timely manner. Good grief! They conveniently (maybe even cleverly) delayed adjudication of the claim, and in doing so deprived my office of the proper amount of time to submit an appeal. They simply timed out the claim and acted as if we had been the ones who kept it in a drawer for over a year.

Incorrect Coordination of Benefits

This is one of the more complicated and frustrating issues to deal with. It can arise when you submit a claim for a patient who has insurance coverage through multiple plans.

Many patients have more than one insurance carrier for health insurance coverage. One plan will be designated as the primary plan and the others will be designated as secondary, tertiary, etc. Then there are those times when a patient has their insurance plan but carries and uses their spouse's plan, too. Sometimes the patient's plan is the primary one, and other times, the spouse's plan is the primary one. Confused? You are not alone. It can get quite tangled up.

Unfortunately, many patients don't know the order in which their coverage stacks up, and for that matter, neither do the insurance carriers. In such cases, it is up to your office to figure this out. And your office can easily end up stuck in the middle of a dispute between two (or more) insurance companies, both (or all) of which are good at playing a little game called "Let's wait it out and see if the other party will fold and pay the bill."

Other times, an insurance company won't adjudicate a claim until the patient completes a survey or confirms that their insurance coverage has not changed. Here again, there is nothing you can do but wait for this to play out. Some insurance companies take great advantage of this administrative option and make this the default response on all claims.

Every doctor has his or her exasperating story of that one claim (or maybe more) that took forever to be processed and reimbursed. For me, the longest I ever had to wait to be reimbursed for a service was SIX years. And by that time, my patient had already passed away.

These are just a few of the many roadblocks you might encounter along the course of your Revenue Collections Cycle. **Getting paid for the services you perform should not be this difficult**; unfortunately, when you rely on third-party payors for payment, you have no control over how much you will be paid or when you will receive payment. There are simply too many factors that are completely out of your control. That's why medical practices need to stay on top of their Revenue Collection Cycle and closely monitor the processing of claims.

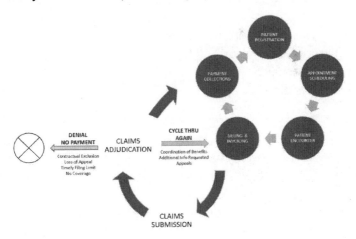

Figure 6. In an insurance-based practice, claims adjudication can result in 1 of 3 outcomes that are controlled by the third-party payor.

Simply put, the claims adjudication process will end in 1 of 3 outcomes. Either the claim will be paid, the doctor will be asked to provide additional information, or the claim will be denied. Of course, payment of the claim is the ideal outcome. The second outcome—being asked for additional information—is not a denial of the claim, and that's good, but it does prolong the Revenue Collection Cycle beyond what is ideal. Then there is the third outcome: denial of the claim. Denials can be handled in 1 of 3 ways. You can appeal the claim, you can bill the patient for the service, or you can write off the service as a loss.

You must monitor the health of your Revenue Collection Cycle! You must take all steps possible on your end to ensure you get reimbursed accurately and in a timely fashion. This is not an area of your practice to put on autopilot and walk away. You might have to set up a process for reviewing the claims and this might involve adjusting your internal processes. No matter how much oversight you create on your end, however, you must also be aware of this basic—and unfortunate—fact: once you submit a claim, you no longer have control over the process and, from that point on, you are dependent on someone else to determine the outcome. And to that extent, the Cash Flow (a metric that will be discussed in the next chapter) can be hard to predict.

This has been a long chapter—the longest chapter in the book—and for good reason. If you didn't already, you should now be recognizing and coming to terms with how the obstacles inherent in an insurance-based model make it nearly impossible for a medical practice to achieve a highly efficient and reliable Revenue Collection Cycle. One that doesn't tie up your staff with endless paperwork and time spent on hold with insurance companies. One that is, let's say—using our previous digestion analogy—not bloated, constipated, and irritable.

So, how can we eliminate these hiccups and snags? How can we resolve this condition? Is there an alternative?

I think you know my answer—**YES THERE IS!**

Get Rid Of The Third-Party Payors!

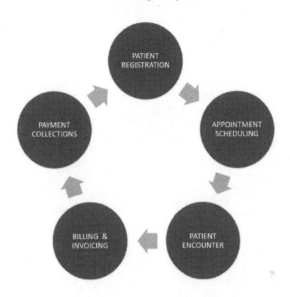

Figure 7. A revenue collection cycle in a Direct Care private practice is closed to any third-party intervention.

We already know that this cycle has 5 steps in total and 2 easily managed processes: billing and payment. And payment is received before the patient leaves the office, just as it is in our hotel example earlier. No phone calls to insurance companies. No coding. No denials and appeals. No waiting indefinitely for payment.

Direct Care Medicine eliminates the third-party payor and all the insurance requirements.

From an operations standpoint, breaking free from third-party insurers accrues the following benefits:

- It streamlines the process.

- It creates efficiency within the system.

- It alleviates the uncertainty of Cash Flow.

And it preserves precious resources:

- Your time.

- Your staff's time.

- Your patient's time.

Best of all, when you cut out all that minutia, you can get back to focusing on patient care. It's a win-win for both you and your patients!

So, let's get back to our discussion of the Key Performance Indicators of your practice. The next chapter, as I mentioned, is dedicated to Cash Flow. By now I am sure you understand the difference between Revenue and Cash Flow and are ready to take a look at some Cash Flow KPIs.

CHAPTER 8

CASH FLOW METRICS

So here we are now getting down to the business of Cash Flow—a *make-it-or-break-it* topic. As I've pointed out several times so far, many people confuse Revenue and Cash Flow. But, if you've gotten this far in the book, you are no longer one of those people. You now see how your practice can be booking a large amount of Revenue but then (through no fault of your own) not convert all of that Revenue to Cash. You see how it's possible for your schedule to be booked solid and for you to be working breathlessly to see all those patients and still come up short of cash when it comes time to pay bills. This all seems counterintuitive, right? But after reading the previous chapter on the Revenue Collection Cycle of an insurance-based medical practice, you now realize the potential roadblocks and pitfalls of the insurance-based business model.

Managing the Cash Flow of an insurance-based medical practice requires diligent oversight. There are a few KPIs you need to know and track to assess the liquidity of your business. Keeping an eye on these numbers will help you maintain the balance between cash flowing into the practice and cash flowing out of the practice.

Accounts Receivable Aging Report

As we established, patients don't always pay their portion at the time of service. And we know that insurance companies don't pay their portion at the time of service. So, when you provide your service to a patient and book Revenue as having been earned, that amount shows up as an Account Receivable entry on your books. Accounts Receivable is a bookkeeping term. It represents the amount of money earned by you and payable to you—to be received at some time in the future in the form of cash.

We measure the quality of Accounts Receivable management by the length of time it takes to turn over the receivable or, in other words, convert the receivable to cash. If you book Revenue in Accounts Receivable on the first of the month and you collect cash for it on the first of the next month, then the turnover on that receivable is one month or 30 days. An Accounts Receivable Aging Report will tell you how old, on average, the receivables on your books are: one month (30 days), two months (60 days), three months (90 days), etc. Your goal is to minimize the time it takes to collect for your services. In other words, you don't want your Accounts Receivable to be 90 days old. Your Accounts Receivable Aging Report will tell you just how well you are doing in that regard.

Keep an eye on the number of days it takes to collect payments from individual patients and insurance companies. Tracking this metric will allow you to assess the efficiency of your billing and collections processes. The shorter the collection period, the better your Cash Flow position will be. By reducing the number of days in Accounts Receivable, you can improve your practice's liquidity and its ability to cover financial obligations promptly.

One Doctor's Story – Accounts Receivable

I had a cardiologist reach out and ask me to help him evaluate and analyze his Revenue Collection Cycle. His office manager had told him the practice's bottom line was just fine. Trusting his office manager, he had never felt compelled to delve into the matter.

I walked him through his cycle, starting at the point where a patient booked an appointment and ending at the point where his practice received payment for the service provided. In doing so, we noticed that his practice was experiencing a significant delay in collecting payment for services rendered. There was a bottleneck somewhere. But where? To figure this out, we had to review every step in the cycle.

Using his practice management software, we generated an aging report. This report revealed an alarming number of denials over 90 days old. We looked further and discovered that many of the denials were related to incorrect patient demographics. If you recall from the last chapter, patient demographics are collected during the first step of the cycle when the patient makes an appointment. Once the doctor identified this weak link in his cycle, he was able to address it. He set up a protocol to ensure consistency of patient information intake and input into the system.

Another glitch we found involved the submission of secondary claims. It turns out, everyone in the office assumed these claims were all being forwarded to the clearinghouse. This was not the case, but it was only discovered through our review process. Once the doctor realized this breakdown in the process, he created a protocol for staff members to review all secondary claims to make sure they got submitted properly.

Unfortunately, not all secondary claims were being recuperated. The thought of that lost opportunity weighed heavily on the doctor. He hired a new office manager to go over the numbers with him. (A reminder that no one will look after your money better than you.) He set a short-term goal of reducing the average age of accounts receivable from 90 days to 30 days and was able to achieve this goal by addressing the bottlenecks we discovered.

By reviewing the Accounts Receivable Aging Report and then analyzing the Revenue Collections Cycle of his practice, this doctor was able to identify problems that were negatively affecting the liquidity of his practice. Once he knew what the problems were, he was able to come up with solutions, improve the cash flow into his practice and enhance its financial stability as well.

Accounts Payable Aging Report

Just like a restaurant owner needs to manage payments to its suppliers, your practice needs to manage payments to its creditors. Your goal here is to hold onto your cash as long as possible without penalty. When it comes to Accounts Receivable, you want the receivables to be converted to cash as quickly as possible. But when it comes to Accounts Payable, you want to negotiate the most favorable terms possible for your practice—the longer, the better.

If your receivables, on average, are turning over every 90 days, but you have 30-day terms on your payables, well, you might run into what is called a "cash crunch." That's when you haven't yet brought into practice the amount of cash you need to pay out to your creditors. The cash is "in the mail," so to speak, but your creditor is banging on your door demanding payment now.

This is a very unpleasant situation. It's also very draining for a doctor. Doctors want to give their time and energy to their patients. They don't want to be lying awake at night haunted by the demands of creditors. I hope you can see that it's not just the doctor who suffers in this situation. It's the patients, too. When doctors are burdened by financial chaos, they simply don't have as much of themselves to give to their patients. Everyone loses here.

This is why it is important to monitor both the total amount of Accounts Payable as well as the length of time you must meet those obligations—also known as an Accounts Payable Aging Report. Keeping a close eye on these Metrics can help you effectively manage your financial obligations—in the manner most advantageous to your practice. You want to optimize your payment schedules by negotiating the most favorable terms possible with suppliers. This might surprise you, but it is possible to maintain good business relationships and at the same time maximize the cash you have available for expenses. No one is happy when a business fails. Success for one leads to success for others in a free market system.

Collections

Collections are the payments you receive from patients, insurance companies, or other sources. Think of it as the money hitting the cash register in a restaurant. This is money that is "in hand" or within your grasp to use. Monitoring your collections allows you to track the actual funds coming into your practice. This metric helps you ensure that your revenue is being converted into cash effectively, enabling you to manage your cash flow, meet financial obligations, and make timely decisions about investments or expenses.

Operating Cash Flow

Operating cash flow is the sum of money that your practice generates or spends on daily activities. In simplest terms, it is the net financial ins and outs from any of the primary services - including patient visits, treatments, procedures, and operating costs.

However, when you are first starting, or if you are anticipating a change in revenue coming into your practice, you must have a backup source of money to cover the operating cash flow.

As I tell clients, it is important to anticipate these lulls and be prepared because you still have expenses to meet and pay - things like rent, salaries, the light bill, and your medical supply vendors.

Many practices will typically secure backup monies through local banks in the form of business loans or lines of credit. Oftentimes, banks have special programs for medical practices, which can include customized loan options, working capital lines of credit, or financing options for equipment. Additional alternative options for some medical practices include Angel Investors, crowdfunding and joint ventures or partnerships.

For monies that are through loans, lines of credit, or financing, you must understand the interest rates, repayment schedules, and all the terms of the contract.

CHAPTER NINE

PATIENT METRICS

Patient metrics have much the same impact as customer metrics on a restaurant. For doctors to increase income, workload, and business growth, they must understand patient volume, average revenue per patient, patient retention rate, and patient referral rate.

Patient Volume

Patient volume refers to the number of patients your medical practice serves within a specific period, just like the number of customers a restaurant serves within a given period. Physicians need to know their patient volume and how it directly impacts the total revenue and workload of the practice.

I advise my clients to start by setting goals for patient volume, both monthly and quarterly. Then, based on the results they achieve over these periods, I help them create strategies to retain those patients and attract new ones. It doesn't matter how great your services are. If you don't have a robust patient volume, you won't have much of a business.

Average Revenue per Patient

Average Revenue per Patient is the average amount of revenue generated from each patient visit, similar to the average spending per customer in a restaurant. As you begin monitoring this number, get in the habit of making a connection between each patient encounter and its financial impact on your business. Also, start thinking in terms of potential for revenue growth.

You do this by looking for opportunities during patient visits to provide value-added services and to upsell or cross-sell relevant medical services. With each patient visit, you have both a captive audience and adjunct services to offer. Don't waste the opportunity. For example, as part of tendinitis treatment, you can consider an additional in-office analgesic product or a series of in-office physical therapy treatments that would increase the revenue generated for that patient at that particular visit.

Patient Retention Rate

Patient Retention Rate measures the percentage of patients who continue to seek care from your practice over time. Just like a restaurant will strive to turn each new customer into a loyal, repeat customer, physicians should also strive to build a base of loyal patients. Not only do loyal patients represent regular revenue for your office, but they also often become ambassadors for your practice by spreading the word to their friends and colleagues. You'd be surprised at how many people like to brag about their doctors, as in "My doctor is better than your doctor." You can count it all as free advertising.

Patient retention is not only important for continuity of care but also for the financial stability of your practice. I remind my physician clients that the Patient Retention Rate directly reflects the quality of patient communication and the strength of their doctor-patient relationship. This metric is something every Direct Care physician should be closely following and always trying to improve. Take the time to understand your patient's needs, practice active listening, and address all concerns or feedback when it's shared. This is the way to foster long-term relationships.

Patient Referral Rate

The patient referral rate measures the number of new patients who come to your practice as a result of recommendations from existing patients and referrals from healthcare entities. Just like a restaurant will benefit from word-of-mouth recommendations and advertising, physicians can leverage patient referrals to expand their patient base. As we have already stated, attracting patients is critical. By implementing specific strategies and providing resources and tools, you can effectively track, monitor, and improve patient metrics while delivering high-quality care and fostering your patient loyalty.

Monitoring Patient Metrics—One Doctor's Story

I had a sports medicine physician request a practice analysis. One of the things he was concerned with was the fluctuating patient volume in his practice. Some weeks he would be overwhelmed with appointments, while other weeks his practice seemed unusually slow. I worked with him on analyzing his patient metrics and showed him how monitoring these metrics can help him make strategic decisions about his schedule.

We started with a specific time frame and tallied the number of appointments per week, noting the types of procedures performed. Once we had this data, we were able to study it for patterns and trends. It was evident that there were seasonal variations in patient volume, so we looked for factors that might be contributing to those variations. The local school's sports seasons were impacting the fluctuations in patient volumes. At the beginning of each season, his patient volume went up.

We then took a look at the external factors that were contributing to the lulls in his practice such as holidays and school breaks. Knowing this, we then brainstormed ways to counter the impact of these external factors on his patient volume with strategic measures such as implementing internal marketing initiatives, boosting his referral networks, and stepping up patient outreach programs. Of course, I advised him to track the results of these countermeasures so he could allocate his resources (time and money) effectively going forward. With all this information in hand, we discovered that there were certain times during the year when lulls would be inevitable. Even this information was valuable from a planning perspective for it allowed this doctor to pinpoint the slower periods on his calendar where he could potentially take a vacation without significantly impacting patient care.

Patient Retention Rate was another metric this doctor and I studied for insight. It revealed how many of his patients returned for follow-up appointments or additional therapy treatments. This, I explained to him, was one way to measure patient satisfaction with his practice. It also helped him identify those patients most likely to refer new patients to his practice.

The insights this physician gained from monitoring his patient metrics and understanding the office dynamics were eye-opening. Not only did the review of patient metrics help him feel more in control of his practice's operations, but it also helped him realize the importance of proactively managing patient volume for maintaining a healthy work-life balance.

CHAPTER 10

INSURANCE METRICS

As you transition out of an insurance-based model, you can avoid financial instability by planning your exit from your contracts carefully and strategically. This includes analyzing each payor's reimbursement rates, denial rates, and reimbursement time.

Average Reimbursement per Procedure

The Average Reimbursement per Procedure represents the amount of money you receive from insurance companies for each specific medical procedure or service provided. You can gather this data using your practice management software. Simply look up the respective CPT code and make note of the reimbursement amount as a whole and per insurance carrier. This metric directly impacts your practice's Total Revenue and profitability, so you must become familiar with it. Once you do, you will be able to identify low reimbursement rate procedures as well as the insurance companies that reimburse poorly. Armed with this information, you will then be able to be more selective about which insurance plans you allow into your practice and which procedures you prioritize.

Insurance Denial Rate

Insurance Denial Rate measures the percentage of claims that are denied or rejected by insurance companies. High denial rates can result in delayed or reduced reimbursements and negatively impact your practice's cash flow. You will want to train and work closely with your billing and administrative staff to identify common denial reasons and implement strategies for improvement.

Average Time for Reimbursement

Average Time for Reimbursement refers to the time it takes for your medical practice to receive payment from an insurance company after submitting a claim. Lengthy reimbursement cycles can strain your practice's cash flow and create financial challenges. In training sessions, educate physicians about the importance of monitoring and reducing the average time to reimbursement.

Analyzing Insurance and Reimbursement metrics plays a huge role in deciding whether to stay with the insurance model or transition to a non-insurance model. The importance of monitoring Insurance and Reimbursement Metrics cannot be overstated. The financial stability and profitability of your practice depend upon it. By closely examining average reimbursement rates, denial rates, and reimbursement time, you gain insights into the financial impact of insurance contracts on your practice's revenue.

Now, I am biased, and as you know, I promote transitioning to a non-insurance model. Direct Care offers several potential benefits for the financial stability of your practice. By eliminating the complexities and administrative burdens associated with insurance billing and reimbursement, you can achieve greater control over your pricing, increase revenue per patient, and reduce administrative costs. Your practice can respond and adjust to market pressures. Additionally, transitioning to a non-insurance model can enhance patient-provider relationships, streamline operations, and potentially improve overall patient satisfaction.

By monitoring average reimbursement rates, reducing denial rates, and optimizing the time to reimbursement, physicians can ensure a financially stable and profitable practice. However, transitioning to a non-insurance model may offer additional financial benefits, allowing for greater control, increased revenue, and improved patient-provider relationships. Careful evaluation and planning are essential to determine the best approach for your practice's long-term financial stability.

CHAPTER ELEVEN

PUTTING IT ALL TOGETHER

Congratulations on making it to the end of Section Two. We covered a lot of material. With each chapter, I hope I was able to make you a bit more comfortable with the KPIs of a medical practice and a bit more aware of the power you will possess when you master them.

Before we leave this subject and move on to Section Three, I would like to touch on a few final topics regarding the numbers.

There are three basic financial statements all business owners must learn to read: the income statement, the balance sheet, and the cash flow statement. I will provide you with a brief overview of these three statements, as well as a basic understanding of what you can learn about the financial condition of your practice from each one. Then there is the matter of Return on Investment. That's a financial ratio every business owner needs to understand, so before we leave our discussion of the numbers behind, I'll make sure you are aware of that one too.

Financial Reports

Reviewing your practice's overall financial condition every quarter is a fairly reasonable goal to set for yourself. You can do this by looking at three basic financial statements: your practice's income statement, its balance sheet, and its cash flow statement. (Many practices coordinate this review process with their accountants around the time they file their business taxes.)

Financial statements are valuable in many ways:

- They provide you with an overview of how your practice is performing financially and they allow you to identify trends, spot areas for improvement, and make informed decisions to optimize revenue and minimize expenses.

- They play a critical role in complying with legal and regulatory requirements by providing transparency and a record of your practice's financial transactions. Both are necessary for tax filings, audits, potential partnerships, and/or collaborations.

- They are practical, insightful, and valuable, particularly when it comes to managing your practice's cash flow.

The *income statement* is considered a snapshot of your practice's financial performance because it sums up activity over a specific period: a month, quarter, or year. The income statement breaks down your revenue into all the various sources of income for your practice. It also details all the expenses of your practice, including COGS and operating expenses. The income statement will reveal whether your practice has made a profit or operated at a loss during the specified period.

The *balance sheet* provides a comprehensive look at your practice's financial position at one specific point in time. The balance sheet has three components to it: assets, liabilities, and equity. The sum of all assets will be equal to the sum of all liabilities plus equity.

Total assets are broken down on the balance sheet into separate line items for individual asset categories such as cash, accounts receivable, inventory, medical equipment, property, etc. Total liabilities are broken down into separate line items for individual liability categories such as accounts payable, short-term and long-term debt, and taxes owed. Equity represents the portion of the practice's value that belongs to the owners.

Looking at your balance sheet will allow you to gauge your practice's liquidity by checking your cash and other short-term assets (primarily accounts receivable) position versus your short-term liability position. The more liquid your assets are, the better equipped you will be to meet your financial obligations and the more solvent your business will be overall.

The *cash flow statement* focuses on the inflows and outflows of cash within your practice over a given period. It breaks down cash flow into three different activities: operating cash flow, investing activities, and financing activities. Operating cash flow includes cash coming in from various payors for services rendered and cash going out for bills. Remember the difference between income and cash flow. Don't forget, for insurance-based practices, revenue listed on the income statement does not automatically translate into cash coming in on the cash flow statement. Until the revenue is collected in the form of cash, it is accounted for as an account receivable on the balance sheet. See how all three statements come together?

Investing activities on the cash flow statement can be either positive or negative. Cash investment in long-term assets such as medical equipment represents an outflow of cash from an investment activity (negative). The sale of a long-term asset such as property represents an inflow of cash from an investment activity (positive).

Financing activities on the cash flow statement track the flow of cash in and out of the business associated with financing. This would include funding from business loans and equity payments as well as the repayment of such obligations. By understanding how money enters and leaves your practice, you can make sure you have enough cash on hand to meet costs and entertain new ideas for growth. To do this, you must know how to read a cash flow statement.

Return on Investment (ROI)

ROI = ((Net Profit - Initial Investment) / Initial Investment) x 100

Return on Investment (ROI) measures the profitability of an investment relative to its cost. For example, you may consider investing in new medical equipment, expanding your practice, or implementing technology solutions. By calculating the ROI for these investments, you can assess their potential financial returns and make informed decisions that align with your business goals.

Best Practices for Financial Monitoring

Make it a priority to **review and analyze financial reports consistently**. Set aside dedicated time, such as a monthly or quarterly meeting, to review key financial metrics with your staff. Look at revenue, expenses, profitability, and other relevant indicators. Identify trends, compare against benchmarks, and discuss any significant changes. Regularly reviewing and analyzing financial reports allows you to stay on top of your practice's financial performance and make informed decisions. By dedicating time to this process, you demonstrate your commitment to the financial stability of the practice and empower your staff to be financially aware of issues as they arise.

Consider seeking *guidance from financial advisors or consultants* who specialize in the healthcare industry. These professionals can offer valuable insights, help you interpret financial data, and provide recommendations tailored to your practice's needs. They can assist with financial planning, optimizing revenue cycle management, identifying cost-saving opportunities, and navigating complex financial regulations.

Collaborating with experts in this field can bring fresh perspectives and enhance your financial decision-making.

Conduct regular staff training on financial awareness. This will promote a shared understanding and responsibility for the financial well-being of your practice with everyone that works in your practice. It will empower your staff to contribute to the practice's financial success and will foster a collaborative environment where everyone is aligned toward common goals.

Remember, financial monitoring is an ongoing process that requires consistent effort and attention. By implementing these best practices, you create a foundation for effective financial management of your private practice. Promote a sense of financial awareness among your team, ensure regular review and analysis of financial reports, and seek expert guidance when needed. This approach will help you make informed decisions, improve financial stability, and ultimately support the long-term success of your practice.

However, consider this—

When you convert to a Direct Care model, the approach to financial monitoring will undergo significant changes. FOR THE BETTER! Without the complexities of insurance reimbursements and contracts, you'll have more control over your pricing, revenue streams, and financial operations.

The way that you approach financial monitoring in a cash and Direct Care practice will change.

The shift will create ***simplified financial metrics***. Your primary focus will be on tracking revenue generated directly from patient payments. You will continue to monitor key metrics such as patient volume, average revenue per patient, and revenue by service type. These metrics will give you a clear picture of your practice's financial performance and help you gauge the success of your business.

As you transition away from insurance, you have **stream-lined cost management** because your cost structure changes. Evaluate your overhead costs, staffing needs, and supply expenses to align them with your new business model. Identify areas where you can optimize costs, negotiate better pricing with vendors, and streamline operations to maximize profitability.

The shift to Direct Care provides an opportunity to deliver an **enhanced patient experience**. You can emphasize patient satisfaction. You can monitor patient retention rates, referral rates, and feedback to ensure your patients are receiving value and are willing to pay for your services out of pocket.

During the transition, continue monitoring and analyzing your financial metrics to ensure the financial stability of your practice. As you gain more control over your pricing and revenue streams, you can adjust based on the data to optimize your profitability. Leverage the freedom and flexibility of the cash and Direct Care model to provide personalized care, improve patient satisfaction, and build a sustainable and financially stable practice.

Remember, the transition to cash will require adjustments in your financial monitoring approach, but it also opens up new growth opportunities and increases control over your practice's financial stability.

I encourage you to implement these monitoring practices in your medical private practice. By staying proactive in monitoring your practice's financial performance, you can make informed decisions, seize opportunities, and navigate challenges effectively. Remember, financial stability is the cornerstone of a successful practice, enabling you to provide quality care to your patients while ensuring the sustainability and growth of your business.

SECTION 3

MAKING DECISIONS

"Pay attention to your thoughts and decide whether to continue with them or change them. There is a negative impact when unexamined thoughts run our lives and businesses."
- Dr. Nneke Unachukwu (Dr. Una), pediatrician, CEO of EntreMD and author of *The EntreMD Method*

It's Always About Choices!

In Florida, you are allowed to get your learner's permit to drive a car when you are 15 years old. In my family, the job of driving instructor fell on my dad. He and I would spend afternoons and weekends wheeling around town in the parking lot at the mall or on low-traffic streets. Yellow lights were my Achilles heel. I would freeze up. *Go? Don't Go?* I never felt like I had enough time to make the decision. (Did you—when you were 15?) My mind was simply not used to making split-second decisions with such big consequences on the line.

There were times when I'd see a yellow light and step hard on the gas (vroom!) only to step even harder on the brake one second later (screech!) *Go!* I'd think, followed by *No, don't go!* Then there were times when my first instinct was to break hard followed immediately by a complete opposite impulse to gun it through a light that had turned red already. Whoops.

"What was that?" my dad would ask.

"I don't know," I'd say. "I didn't know what to do."

Fearing he might end up with a whiplash injury, my father gave me some advice I still carry with me decades later. As you approach the yellow light, you have two choices, he said. You can either accelerate and keep going or you can press the brake and wait at the red light. But you can't do both. *Commit or Don't Commit!* he liked to say. Deciding to go forward through a yellow light, he explained, required a full commitment and nothing less. If you can't commit, then stay put and accept the standstill. To this day, as I approach a yellow light, I still hear those words in my head. I recently passed that same advice on to my children when I was teaching them to drive.

This piece of fatherly wisdom has applications beyond safe driving. My dad, a general surgeon, usually had a resident or fellow in his room. I had the opportunity to scrub cases with my dad on occasion and recall hearing him repeat a familiar preliminary interrogation of his surgeons as he handed over the scalpel: "Are you ready? Do you know what you are going to do? Are you sure about where you want to make your incision? If so, then commit! Otherwise, Don't Proceed! Let me have the knife and let's do this together!" Saying this would put surgeons on the spot by forcing them to be honest about their level of conviction. But my dad's ultimate goal was not to rattle his surgeons, it was to help them gain confidence in their ability to commit to their choices. Decision-making is a skill. My father knew how to help people – his children as well as his surgeons - develop this skill. And he knew if a person was not ready to commit to a decision, it was much better for them to pause and wait rather than rush or waiver.

Now that you've reached Section Three–Making Decisions–I'd like to offer you the same advice. When it comes to making your decision about Direct Care Medicine, you can't have it both ways. It's either *Commit!* or *Don't Commit!* You are either in or you are not. It's a binary choice. Are you going to step on the gas and zoom ahead? Or are you going to step on the break and stay put for the time being and make peace with that decision?

If you do decide to go forward with building a Direct Care practice, I am here to share some tools that can help you achieve that goal. Moreover, in addition to what I have to offer, you might be surprised to find a plethora of support available from others who have gone ahead and are eager to help you succeed.

However, in terms of making that initial decision to press the gas or to press the brake, YOU have to do this on your own. No one else can make that decision for you. It all boils down to your personal risk tolerance and your willingness to put in the work to achieve your goal. You are the only one who can evaluate yourself in that regard. It's a highly personal process: a purely subjective one.

Asking yourself some hard questions, probing ones, can help you measure your readiness (or lack of readiness) to commit to making a sweeping change in your business operations. Read through the questions below and allow yourself some time with each one. Notice any tension that might arise in your body. Listen to those or any other sensations that arise. They are feedback.

- Do you find it annoying when insurance companies interfere with your clinical judgment and treatment plans and, in doing so, block the best interests of your patients?

- Do you find it frustrating to spend more time on paperwork and insurance claims than on patient care?

- Do you feel harried by the constant pressure to see more and more patients each day to offset declining reimbursement rates from insurance companies and increasing denials of claims?

- Are you tired of insurance companies denying coverage for necessary treatments or procedures that you believe are medically justified?

- Are you irritated by the ever-changing billing and coding requirements imposed by insurance companies?

- Are you exhausted by the administrative hurdles and delays you encounter when trying to obtain approval from insurance companies for necessary tests or referrals?

More importantly, personally -

- Are you finding it difficult to maintain a healthy work-life balance due to the demands and constraints imposed by insurance-based medicine?

- Have you experienced a sense of frustration or burnout resulting from long working hours and the high patient volumes required to meet insurance company expectations?

- Do you feel that your personal life and well-being have been compromised due to the excessive administrative burdens and paperwork associated with insurance-based medicine?

- Have you contemplated transitioning to a cash-based practice to regain control over your schedule, reduce administrative burdens, and have more autonomy in providing patient care?

If you answered yes to one or more of those questions, you might be a strong candidate for moving forward. If, on the other hand, you didn't answer yes to a single one, then you might not be a strong candidate for Direct Care Medicine. And there's nothing wrong with that. If you are being honest, then that's the best policy. I understand why many of my colleagues stay put and work within the current system with all its flaws. Direct Care Medicine is simply not the right choice for them, and that is OK!

Just remember, as traffic signals cycle and red lights turn green, you can always decide to move forward in the future. In the meantime, if you decide to sit at the red light, please remember my dad's advice. Make peace with your decision to stay put. Use the time to gather more information, talk to more doctors who have transitioned, and further examine the impact the broken system is having on you, your staff, and your patients. But please keep this book with you as a reminder that there is another way.

Having grown up along the waters of the Gulf of Mexico, there's a saying we use quite often: *It's time to fish or cut bait*. So, what's it going to be?

CHAPTER 12

WHERE THERE'S A WILL, THERE'S A WAY

You've taken a look at the KPIs of your practice, you've examined your risk profile, asked yourself tough questions, and pondered your choices. And, after careful consideration, you've decided to press the gas pedal and move ahead on the path toward building a Direct Care practice. You've decided to Commit!

Congratulations! And welcome to a growing community of physicians who are dedicating themselves to reclaiming physician autonomy within the medical profession and restoring the sanctity of the doctor-patient relationship.

Now let's make things happen for you. It's time for you to work smarter. Not harder. In this chapter, I will provide you with the steps and strategies I advise my physician clients to follow as they transition their third-party payor practices to Direct Care models.

The most common questions I get asked when I tell doctors I transitioned in my own practice are the following:

1. *How did you figure out **how** to transition?*

2. *How did you figure out **when** to transition?*

My answer to both of these questions is always the same . . .

It's a PROCESS!

Most private practices will need to transition progressively, over time, out of insurance contracts. Unless you are a start-up or unless a hiatus naturally arises (such as relocation cross-country or extended maternity leave), most physicians cannot quit their insurance plans cold turkey. The time frame for dropping plans varies from practice to practice. Don't judge your success by how quickly your process is moving along. In my case, it took me three years from the day I began dropping contracts to the day I was completely insurance free.

The most important advice I can give you here is to **be strategic**. To transition successfully, to avoid getting out ahead of your skis, so to speak, you must calculate your way over from one business model to the other—one move at a time. It's a chess game of sorts. With each move you make, keep your eye on the KPIs we discussed earlier. Your KPIs will act as warning lights and guide you in your decision-making. *Are you moving too fast? Could you afford to move more quickly?* Check your KPIs for the answers to these and other questions. Over the next few pages, I will explain what I mean by that. I will provide you with the calculations you need to make as you take one step after the next in the right direction.

Moving too quickly or without a strategic vision for success could destabilize the financial health of your practice and place it in jeopardy. Your ultimate goal, in the **long run**, is to be a fully independent Direct Care practice—free from the third-party payor system. Your goal in the **short run**, as you transition over, is to (1) remain in practice and (2) avoid the financial collapse of your business. Remember, you have people who depend upon you: your patients, your family, and your staff.

Turning Lemons into Lemonade

Before we look at the process of transitioning from an insurance-based practice over to a Direct Care practice, I'd like to walk you through a simplified version of changing one business model for another. Something fun and simple. I've chosen that childhood favorite—the lemonade stand.

Some of you might not realize this, but there are kids out there running lemonade stands today who accept credit cards for payment. (Born with the business gene, I guess.) Anyway, let's imagine for a moment that you run one of these lemonade stands that accept credit cards. Only, you've done some quick calculations and have decided it costs you too much money in processing fees. It's just not worth it. You thought you were being cool, but now you realize that old-fashioned cash is the way to go. But there is a small problem. You have an existing base of customers who have become accustomed to paying with a credit card. And you could lose their business when you stop accepting credit card payments.

Is there a way to change the business model of your lemonade stand from cash and credit to cash only without jeopardizing the viability of your business? Yes, there is. You follow the process!

1. You start by determining the current breakdown of lemonade sales between cash and credit. For the sake of this exercise, let's say 50% of your sales are cash and 50% are credit. This will provide you with a worst-case scenario. If it turns out that you cannot convert a single credit card sale to a cash sale (worst case sce-

nario), then you stand to lose 50% of your total sales. Keeping this worst-case scenario in mind, you can prepare your business to weather the downturn in sales by creating a plan to bring your expenses in line with that worst-case revenue number. Knowing what that worst-case number is will provide you with a measure of control. But don't worry. I'm not suggesting you throw up your hands and accept the worst-case revenue number. Indeed not. The next few steps in the process will help you minimize the loss of lemonade sales (and avoid the worst-case scenario) as you transition over. However, even though you will be taking the mitigating steps I'm going to explain, you should have plans in place to bring expenses in line with the worst-case scenario. This will provide you with peace of mind as you venture forth.

2. Once you establish the worst-case scenario, you can then implement various strategies for holding lemonade sales as steady as possible while you transition. For example, no one is forcing you to drop all credit card transactions in one day. You can start the transitioning process off slowly, for example by gradually reducing the number of credit card sales you allow within defined periods. You can reduce this number week by week or month by month or longer. You are in control. It all depends upon the amount of revenue you are willing to forgo in the short run as you pursue the long-term goal. Taking things slowly will allow time for your customers to get used to the new cash-only policy for lemonade. And it will allow time for you to attract new cash-paying customers to fill in the gaps left by those customers who might leave you. And some of them will. Perhaps they are die-hard credit card consumers and just refuse to deal in cash. But many of your credit card paying customers—the ones who love your lemonade—will just need some time to get used

to the new policy and remember to bring cash when they come to your stand. Over time your breakdown between cash sales and credit card sales will gradually shift in favor of cash from 50/50 to 60/40 to 70/30, etc. Keep your eye on Total Revenue as you scale back the credit card transactions and adjust your pace according to how it is impacting revenue.

3. The next strategy you have at your disposal involves incentives. Money is a great motivator. Here are two options for you. You can either encourage customers to pay in cash by offering them a discount on cash payments—say something like 5%. Or you can disincentivize them from using credit cards by charging a processing fee for card payments. The latter option accomplishes two objectives: it discourages the use of credit cards, and it covers the processing fee you have to pay on credit card payments.

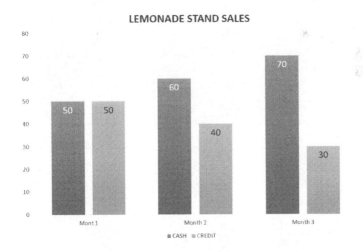

Figure 8. Transitioning from a mixed cash/credit payment to a cash-based model occurs over a period of time in our fictional lemonade stand example.

4. As I mentioned earlier, keep your eye on the ball (the Total Revenue number) at all times. It must always exceed Total Expenses. Establish in advance the minimum amount of Total Revenue you must generate to remain in the lemonade business and adjust the speed of your transition accordingly. Be purposeful and consistent in your pursuit of the new business model. Take strategic but gradual steps to reduce credit card transactions but also make sure expenses are covered. By doing both, you will remain in business and eventually reach your goal of running a pure cash-based lemonade stand.

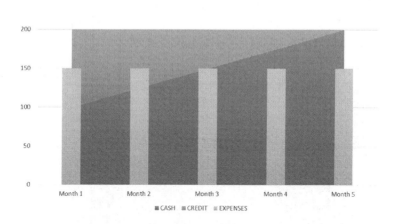

LEMONADE STAND SALES & EXPENSES

Figure 9. As the transition from cash/credit payment to a cash-based model occurs, the business must cover monthly expense.

Same Concept Different Business

This simplified example was designed to help you build a mental framework for understanding the process of transitioning a business from one form of payment to another. Lemonade stands are infinitely less complicated than medical practices, but the basic strategy for successful transitioning is the same.

As a doctor currently running an insurance-based medical practice, you accept payment from your patients in the form of insurance—or, in other words, in the form of the right to claim payment from the patient's insurance company. When you transition your practice over to a Direct Care business model, you will no longer participate with any insurance plans. Because you likely accept multiple insurance plans, you will be exiting multiple insurance plans as you transition. The impact on your business from leaving these plans will vary from plan to plan, depending upon several variables. These variables are what you will consider when creating your transition strategy.

My physician clients find it helpful when I break the process down into two stages: the steps you take to prepare your transition strategy and the steps you take to carry out your transition strategy.

In the **first stage**, you will gather crucial data, information, and statistics such as the number of plans you accept in your practice, the number of patients per plan, and the breakdown of reimbursement rates by plan, among other data. You will use this information to critically assess the financial impact of dropping each plan before you begin the transition.

In the **second stage** of the process, you will crunch the numbers and monitor in real-time the impact of discontinuing contracts as you go. No rule says you have to drop all plans simultaneously. Rather, what you want to do is selectively drop insurance plans in a measured fashion, starting with the least lucrative ones, while keeping an eye on the KPIs of your business and the overall stability of your financial structure. *Steady as you go!* This should be your mantra. To ensure success, you must plan the transition carefully, implement it gradually and monitor the financial metrics closely.

First Stage

You start by gathering the various forms of data and information you will need to create and implement your exit strategy. If you happen to be using practice management software, then there is good news: you can use that software to generate most of these numbers. A billing company can produce the information for you as well. Ask your billing company to provide the information in two forms: the raw data and the reports. Remember, the billing company works for you.

So, are you ready? Here is the information you need to compile before you start making decisions.

Your Revenue Sources

Start at the top by tallying Total Revenue. Then break down the amount each of your carriers contributes to Total Revenue. Also, calculate the revenue that comes into the practice in the form of cash. Cash revenue usually comes from non-covered procedures and in-office products. These revenue numbers provide you with a starting reference point. You need to know how much Total Revenue your practice, operating fully within the third-party payor system, is bringing in and the revenue contribution per source. As you begin exiting various plans, you will use these starting point numbers to calculate the impact of your transition strategy.

Your Total Expenses

The next thing you need to calculate is your Total Expense number. You must take an honest look at how much it costs you each month to run your business. And I'm talking about everything—both your fixed expenses and your variable ones. Be sure to include amounts for taxes, emergencies, and "things I don't know yet" or, in other words, unexpected contingencies. That last number is different for each person, each practice.

Knowing how much it costs you to run your business is just plain common sense. It is Budgeting 101. To make a profit, your Total Revenue must exceed your Total Expenses. Having a solid understanding of Total Expenses will allow you to prepare yourself to handle a "worst-case" revenue scenario. If you know the minimum you need to stay in business, you will be able to pace your exit from the plans according to your financial obligations.

Price List and Fee Schedules

Price lists and fee schedules are not the same thing. Unfortunately, many physicians, including me, fell into the trap of thinking that they were because, in the early years of insurance reimbursement, the physician's price lists were paid in full by the insurance companies. Therefore, there was no difference; however, through the years, insurance companies negotiated reimbursement rates and physicians agreed to fee schedules lower than the full amount to keep patients and stay in the network.

What actually should be happening is that doctors set their prices for visits, procedures, treatments, etc., and create their price lists (think of it like a menu). If you were to call a doctor's office and ask what the price is for a certain procedure, you would be quoted a number from that doctor's price list. Price lists (which we will cover in a later chapter) should be based on 2 fundamental criteria: 1) how much it costs to offer the services and 2) the perceived value of the service by your patient.

Fee schedules are set by insurance companies. Each insurance company has its own fee schedule. Reimbursements for visits, procedures, treatments, etc., can and do vary widely from one insurance company to the next. Doctors are free to set their prices at any level they want; however, they are not allowed to set prices according to the patient's insurance plan. Insurance regulators and practice management advisors tell doctors to maintain a "single fee" to charge all claims sent to contracted carriers. This is where the term becomes incorrectly interchanged. So, if Plan A reimburses doctors $1,000 for treatment X and Plan B reimburses doctors $500 for treatment X, the doctor submits a claim with the same amount to both Plans, and then when reimbursement is adjudicated, the doctor must write off the difference.

Now, once you begin the process of transitioning out of insurance plans, you must continue to use a single charge for your contracted carriers; however, be ready, in case you get asked to explain your separate cash price list. For me, I simply explained to my patients that my cash price was what I offered for same-day payment, and the cash price differed from the insurance price because I have to wait an unknown amount of time to collect any payment on that.

Reimbursement Rates

CPT CODE	DOCTOR'S PRICE LIST	INSURANCE FEE SCHEDULE				
		PLAN A	PLAN B	PLAN C	PLAN D	PLAN E →
Procedure 1						
Procedure 2						
Procedure 3						
Procedure 4						
Procedure 5 ↓ etc.						

Figure 10. Create a chart to compare practice price and insurance reimbursement rate to procedure codes

Go through each insurance carrier and calculate the reimbursement rate for each of your services. For example, look at Plan A and calculate the reimbursement under Plan A for each service you provide. And then do the same thing for Plan B and Plan C and so forth. Make a spreadsheet with the reimbursement rates under each plan. Compare these rates with your current price list for insurance claims. Using this information, determine if the reimbursement rates–plan by plan and procedure by procedure–are sufficient to cover your cost of providing the service (i.e., your expenses, including overhead and administration.)

Primary Contributors to Revenue

You need to know which plans are contributing the most to your Total Revenue. You also must determine the reason why a certain plan is contributing more to your revenue than other plans. That plan might have higher reimbursement rates than other plans. Or, percentage-wise, perhaps more of your patients use that plan than other plans. It would not be wise to impulsively drop a plan based on its reimbursement rates alone. You must first consider how many of your patients use that plan and calculate the impact of losing that revenue.

Once you know the breakdown of your revenue plan by plan, you will be able to make calculated exit decisions. As you start the process of dropping plans, you will want to hold onto the plans that are contributing the most to Total Revenue. And you will want to exit the plans that contribute the least–either because they have lower reimbursement rates or fewer patients in your practice use those plans. You must review the actual contracts of plans you are considering dropping to understand the specific payment rates, requirements for billing and filing, and most importantly, the terms of termination.

The Cost of Administrative Burdens

Let's face it. Some insurance plans are simply easier to work with than others. Some insurance plans make your staff jump through multiple hoops to secure reimbursement–this can include everything from asking for more information to denying claims outright, forcing you, of course, to refile the claims. These kinds of shenanigans– as we discussed in the chapter on the Revenue Collection Cycle–affect your Cash Flow negatively, because they prevent you from getting paid in a timely fashion. And this can negatively impact your Working Cash Flow and force you to access your short-term line of credit. This then generates additional expenses for your practice in the form of interest expense. When making your decisions about which plans to drop, be sure to consider and evaluate the administrative burden of working with each insurance plan. The more difficult the plan is to work with, the easier it will be to say goodbye to them. However, be aware that determining the administrative burden of your plans is not a black-and-white calculation. It will be a subjective calculation and include non-financial factors such as time and frustration.

The Impact of Dropping Contracts

At this point, it's time to play the *what-if* game. Using the information you've gathered so far, run the numbers and see for yourself how dropping each of your carriers–Plan A, Plan B, Plan C, etc.--will affect the financial status of your practice. Estimate the impact on the Total Revenue of each loss. It's natural to assume you will suffer the least by dropping a plan that pays the least and/or has high administrative costs. However, if a large number of your patients use that plan, you won't know for sure what the impact will be until you run the numbers.

Create a financial forecast based on various scenarios. Play around with different possibilities and different combinations. Drop Plan A and Plan D in one scenario. Drop Plan B and Plan C in another. And so on. Look at as many scenarios as possible. What you are looking for is financial feasibility. You are looking for the combination that eases you toward independence in the most stable fashion possible.

Patient Volume Target

You understand that your revenue is based on two things when it comes to patients - the individual coming in and the monies generated by the services rendered. The combination will affect the revenue.

You will want to consider dropping insurance plans that few of your patients have or payors who require a lot of administrative work for a small number of patients.

You will continue to set targets for your patient volume; however, as you replace the number of insurance-contracted patients (particularly the low-paying payors) with cash patients, you will eliminate uncertainty about budgeting and revenue projections.

Second Stage

You have now gathered an arsenal of information to use as you move your way across the chess board, eliminating insurance plans and freeing your practice from third-party payors. Are you going to start taking out chess pieces willy-nilly? No, you are not. You are going to make your moves strategically.

Implement a Gradual Transition

I transitioned this way and recommend this to anyone who is currently in a traditional insurance-based practice. Using the results of your *what-if* scenarios above, begin by dropping the plans that will have the least negative impact on Total Revenue. To offset losses you experience upfront as you drop plans, you can gradually increase fees on your cash-based services. But, with any billing change you make in your practice, I urge you to first communicate the change to your patients and make them aware of the benefits they too will experience as you change your business model.

Monitor Key Metrics

I cannot stress the importance of monitoring your KPIs as you go along. If you are not already in the habit of monitoring your financial reports, that needs to change before you start shaking things up. You need to monitor all your KPIs. And, as you go along, you need to compare them to the KPIs in your forecasted models. Are your actual numbers in line with the forecasted numbers? Are they falling short? Or maybe they are far ahead of your forecast (yay!). Based on your findings, you can adjust your strategy (tweak here or there) to keep your business financially stable.

Keep Open Communications

Once you've identified which insurance plans you are going to drop and in which order, it's essential for you to explain the changes to your patients each step of the way:

- Be honest: Authenticity goes a long way. Explain to your patients that you are transitioning to a Direct Care practice. Explain why you are doing it.

- Educate patients: Some patients will understand how insurance works, but most won't. Educate your patients about how insurance works. Explain to them how the insurance industry acts as a middleman (a meddlesome one at that) and how both doctors and patients can benefit by removing the intermediary. No one will disagree with creating greater transparency or bringing the cost of healthcare under control. These are shared points of interest everyone can agree upon.

- Provide resources: There are so many resources available to help educate patients about the Direct Care model and the dysfunction of our current healthcare system. Start with the Free Market Medical Association, American Association of Physicians & Surgeons, Docs 4 Patient Care, DPC Alliance, and DSC Alliance. Those are only a few to get you started. There are so many more online. (See the Resources at the end of the book too.)

- Offer Payment Plans: When you no longer have an insurance contract dictating your office protocols, you can be creative and offer alternative ways of payment, including payment plans and bartering.

It is important to remind your patients that you are not abandoning them. Patients are prone to feeling this way when doctors drop their insurance plans. Assure them that this is not the case nor is it your intention. Let them know you are not going anywhere and will always be available to see them as patients and that they will always be your priority. Explain to them that your decision is not about them; it's about their insurance plan and how that plan treats you. Let them know that you are no longer willing or able to accept the onerous terms of the insurance plan—that it's no longer a viable option for you and your practice.

Transitioning to a Direct Care practice is a profound change. You must communicate clearly with your patients for their sake and yours. Informed and educated patients can be powerful ambassadors for your practice. They can (and they do) spread the word about what their doctors are doing! And as you will learn soon, talkative patients— those who are also satisfied with their experience—can be a huge asset to your marketing efforts!

SECTION 4

LAUNCHING YOUR DIRECT CARE PRACTICE

"We as physicians can take back control by getting on-stage - learning to practice medicine in a way that will lead to improved patient care and personal job satisfaction."
- Dr. Rebekah Bernard, author of
How to Be a Rock Star Doctor and *Patients At Risk*

In the last two sections, I focused almost exclusively on the business aspect of launching and running a Direct Care practice, and for good reason. If your Direct Care practice isn't successful financially, it won't be successful in all other respects. What do I mean by that? Well, building a Direct Care practice isn't only about doing better financially. It's about doing better for your patients and the profession in general.

Yes, you need to know your KPIs and monitor the finances of your practice—before you transition, while you transition, and after you transition. At the same time, remember, you also need to commit yourself to building a mindset of innovation, physician autonomy, and patient-centered care. Our profession has drifted so far away from those three principles that it's now almost impossible to remember a time when they were the bedrock of private practice medicine. Many of us, however, firmly believe there is still time to restore these basic values and return the profession's focus to those we pledged to serve—our patients. Don't lose sight of that vision!

Direct Care practitioners are indeed, on the one hand, motivated by the idea of working smarter, not harder. But they are equally motivated by the possibility of making a lasting impact on the lives of their patients and the healthcare landscape as a whole. Direct Care physicians are as idealistic as they come. Remember that! Especially when someone tries to suggest you are leaving the insurance-based system for personal gain.

In this final section of the book, we get down to the nitty-gritty of building a thriving Direct Care practice. By the end of this section, you will know how to market your services to the public and build a brand for your practice. You will know what a pricing strategy is and how to use one to set the prices for your services. You will know how to create a transition plan, one that will help you remain steady through the turbulence all start-ups experience.

Marketing. Branding. Pricing. Transition. These are the topics we will cover in Section Four. They are the building blocks for your new Direct Care practice. It's time to start laying a solid and supportive foundation for your vision. It's time to start turning your vision into a reality.

Now before moving on, let me pause now and take a quick moment to emphasize the importance of communicating with your staff and with your patients. Don't expect your staff to have the same drive and excitement about the transition that you have, and don't expect your patients to immediately understand or even care about your business operations just because they are your patients. You should not take anyone's lack of enthusiasm personally or as criticism. No one will feel as emotionally invested in your business as you do. And that's ok. Enthusiasm will spread slowly as staff members and patients experience first-hand the benefits to them of the new system.

I've always taken the approach of *leading by example* and letting my *actions speak for themselves*. It's a matter of *showing* versus *telling*. Don't exhaust yourself with big lectures and long explanations to win people over. Let the new system sell itself through its simplicity and ease of use and improved health outcomes. One does not have to shout the truth for it to be heard.

Keep in mind, in your office, you will be the one most familiar with the idea of Direct Care. You will be the one most likely to know a Direct Care doctor, to have read articles and social media posts. And you will be the one who has had the benefit of reading this book. Do you get my point? Your staff and your patients are not the ones doing the work to educate themselves. You are. They probably feel the pain of the current system, but more likely than not, they have no reason to see any other way of doing things. And why would they, unless they actively sought out new information like you are right now? So, don't get frustrated if, at the beginning, you encounter an enthusiasm gap between you and your staff and patients. This gap can be closed. It will simply require a little bit of effort on your part, followed by a measure of patience.

Here's the bottom line: to transition successfully to a Direct Care practice you will have to bring your staff and your patients on board with your vision, even if they don't make it easy for you to win them over. You will be creating new protocols to streamline your operations, and new protocols to smooth the transition from one model to the other. These new protocols—as well as the reason for the protocols—must be thoroughly explained to your staff and your patients.

The effectiveness of your communication efforts will be evident in the feedback you receive. The better you are at communicating the vision, the more enthusiasm and support you will generate. In the meantime, as you work to gain support, keep your expectations realistic. Understand that building a successful practice takes time, dedication, and patience.

The last chapter of Section Four will focus on your business plan. A business plan is a comprehensive blueprint for building a business. It's like the blueprint architects use when constructing their buildings. Your business plan will state your goals and objectives for your practice. It will define your strategies and lay out your financial projections. It will serve as a compass to keep you on track and guide your decisions as you go forward.

Remember, bumps along the road will be inevitable. The chapters in Section Four are meant to serve as a roadmap along this bumpy road—to help you stay on course, boost your confidence, and overcome challenges that come your way.

Ready to take the wheel?

CHAPTER 13

YOUR MARKETING STRATEGY

There are many marketing books available in bookstores and libraries–pages upon pages of advice dedicated to helping business owners design a marketing strategy. However, it's been my experience that doctors, for some reason, don't feel called to read these books. When I work with physician clients, I keep this in mind and try my best to explain marketing in the most relatable terms possible. I'll try to do the same here with you.

But before I get going on this topic, let me first address the elephant in the room: the very concept of marketing a medical practice can make many doctors break out in hives. You might be one of them, because I was and used to think that - *Marketing is for things like cars and sodas, not medical care!*

It's normal to feel a little bit uncomfortable with self-promotion. This is a common feeling for people of all professions, not just ours. It certainly would be nice if a person's work could speak for itself without any need to draw attention to it. But that's not the world we live in. Your potential patients are busy people. They don't have time to figure out who you are, where you are, and what you do. They need you to reach out to them with your message.

If some doctors remain stubbornly opposed to marketing their services, it is possible they haven't taken the time to understand the true purpose of marketing, which is **to serve the needs of patients**. Warped perceptions of marketing are embedded in the conditioning doctors receive during their medical training. We are fed a certain message about marketing. We are told not to worry about it. We are told that as long as we are listed in the insurance networks, the patients will find us. No marketing is necessary. See how that hook got baited?

For many doctors, the idea of marketing themselves and their practices feels too much like bragging or being self-absorbed or narcissistic. But hold on a minute! Can we all agree that there are people in the general public who could be helped by your talents and skills? That people are suffering (needlessly), completely unaware that anything can be done to relieve their suffering. How, may I ask, are these people supposed to know that you exist if you don't make an effort to reach out to them? Do you see how your mindset shifts when you flip the perspective from serving yourself to serving others?

Keep these people—the people in need of your services—in mind when you create your marketing strategy. You haven't met them yet, but they exist. Your job now is to open a line of communication to them through a marketing strategy. To let them know you exist, you care, and you want to help. You **can** help! So, is this bragging? Or is this outreach? Unless people everywhere all of a sudden develop telepathy, people who need you will not find you without you making an effort to reach them through a marketing strategy.

Do you remember early on how I talked about the old mindset of insurance-based medicine versus the new mindset of Direct Care Medicine? I said, before you can even begin to transition to a Direct Care practice, you must first work on developing a Direct Care mindset. Well, if at this point you are feeling resistant to creating a marketing strategy, stop and ask yourself *why*? Perhaps you are still under the sway of the old mindset? If so, it might help you to review Chapter Four–Mental Conditioning Matters.

Never lose sight of the fact that Direct Care Medicine is a win-win approach to providing healthcare, with the sanctity of the doctor-patient relationship firmly at its core. Right now, the only ones "winning" in our current healthcare system are the third-party intruders, profit-oriented businesses, by the way, who (you can be sure) work hard day in and day out on their marketing strategies! And now you are going to do the same. Just because you are a doctor, don't for a second fall into a trap of false modesty and form counterproductive beliefs about marketing strategies. When you know better, you can do better. And now you know better.

For the record, in case it's a concern, let me make one thing clear. A successful marketing strategy will never be built on the back of compromised clinical care, for ***clinical care must always be paramount***–the core purpose of your practice. Altering the clinical care, you provide for the sake of financial gain will only undermine your marketing efforts. A successful marketing strategy relies on your clinical care being exceptional, rising above that of your peers. How will this be true if you cut corners?

With the advent of social media, this doesn't change. It is important to realize that social media is just another avenue to connect with your patients and their communities. Social media allows for myriad opportunities to share valuable information with patients, to educate and engage with them; however, the ultimate goal should be the enhancement of patient care rather than the splashy promotion of your practice

Now you know what a marketing strategy isn't. It's not voodoo or a carnival act or a con job or an ego trip. It's none of those things.

So, what is a marketing strategy? A marketing strategy is a progression of intentional steps you take to build your brand and promote your business offerings to a defined market demographic.

In plain terms, marketing is the process by which a business:

- Identifies its Target Market: those consumers who can benefit from its products and/or services.

- Attracts the attention of its Target Market.

- Promotes itself and its offerings to its Target Market.

If a business doesn't market itself, consumers won't know it exists. They won't know what the business has to offer them in terms of products, services, and/or solutions to their problems. Imagine a world in which the Ford Motor Company had not marketed its Model-T, White Castle had not marketed its hamburger, Quaker Oats Company had not marketed its puffed wheat and Apple Inc. had not marketed the Apple-1 personal computer. We may never have known about their products. And those industries—auto, fast food, cereal, and personal computer—might not be what they are today.

A Direct Care medical practice needs a marketing strategy to attract, maintain and sustain a steady stream of patients. Once it has been designed and adopted, your marketing strategy will also function as a guide to continue growing your business. Let's go a little deeper now and look at a few key definitions.

Marketing Fundamentals

These are the fundamental building blocks of an effective marketing strategy.

Target Market

Your Target Market includes anyone who could benefit from your services. It's the population of people who are suffering from the problems that you solve. The people who want their problems solved and are looking for someone to help them. And because you are a Direct Care practitioner, your Target Market will be a specific subset of that population. It will be the people within that population who are seeking alternatives to the insurance-based medical experience.

So, to recap, as a Direct Care physician, your Target Market will be the people who are suffering from the problems you can solve and who are looking for a better healthcare experience than what they've so far encountered within the insurance-based system.

Once you understand who the Target Market for your Direct Care practice is in general, the next step is to create a profile of the Target Market for your practice in particular. This will require some research. You will start by looking at the patients you already have in your practice. Ask questions. Review the answers. As you do this, a picture will begin to emerge of the ideal client for your business: the client who needs your services wants your services, appreciates your services, and is willing to pay for your services.

You begin with the demographics—the basic objective characteristics of your patient base.

- What is the age range of your patients? Do you see more pediatrics or geriatrics?

- What about the gender breakdown—what percentage of your patients is male? What percentage is female?

- Where do your patients live? Are they concentrated in a specific neighborhood, or do they reside across various regions?

- What is the level of education among your patients?

- What is the average income of your patient base?

Next, you look at the psychographics of your patient base—their motivations for seeking out your services. What are their primary reasons for choosing your practice? What values and beliefs do your patients hold and how do they affect their healthcare decisions? Are they focused on holistic care, traditional medicine, or some other approach? Are your patients generally health-conscious? Do they prioritize preventive care, or do they tend to be more reactive when it comes to health issues?

After looking at who your patients are, where they are, and why they come to see you, the next step is to look at what type of treatments or services your patients prefer: consultations, treatment modalities, procedures, etc. Ask yourself, what are the most common health issues they face? How often do they purchase products from your practice?

Lastly, you must investigate what your patients are looking for in their physician. What qualities or attributes do they value? What kind of experience do your patients expect from your practice? Is there anything they particularly appreciate or is there something they wish to see improved? What are some common reasons why your patients might leave a practice? (Often overlooked, the negative preferences can be as insightful as the positive ones.)

As you go through the process of collecting this information, you will begin to recognize patterns and similarities among your patient base. The profile of an ideal patient will emerge. Keep this ideal patient in mind when it comes time to design your marketing strategy.

People who seek care from a Direct Care practitioner tend to have a few things in common in terms of preferences and concerns. They typically agree with the following statements:

- I am seeking high-quality, personalized care at an affordable cost.

- I am dissatisfied with the traditional healthcare system.

- I am seeking more control over my healthcare experience.

Pay attention when you hear these types of views expressed. These are the people who make up your Target Market.

Value Proposition

Your Value Proposition is an articulation of all that your practice provides value to the patient.

Direct Care physicians offer enormous value to their patients that insurance-based practitioners will never be able to match. *I cannot emphasize enough how much of an advantage you have over doctors in insurance-based practices.*

Your Value Proposition will be a crucial part of determining your prices. It's what sets you apart from other doctors, and it's all the reasons why a patient would decide you are worth the price they agree to pay. So put yourself in the patient's shoes. Why would they exchange their money for your services? Because, in their mind, the service you provide is equal in value to the money they give you. It's an exchange of one thing of value for another. No one needs to explain the value of a dollar. But you do need to explain the value of your services.

Here are a few things to consider when you are defining your Value Proposition:

Quality of Care: In what ways do you make sure your patients receive high-quality care? Do you offer longer appointment times and/or personalized treatment plans? Do you use cutting-edge technology?

Convenience: In what ways do you make it easy for patients to see you and receive care? Do you offer flexible appointment times, telemedicine options, and/or same-day appointments?

Customer Service: In what ways do you make your patients feel valued? Do you have a friendly and welcoming staff? Do you provide prompt responses to patient inquiries? Do you provide follow-up calls to check on patients after tests, procedures or to simply ask about their well-being?

Cost Savings: In what ways do you help your patients save money on healthcare? Do you offer bundled pricing for multiple services, transparent pricing, or a membership model that provides access to care at a lower cost?

In the midst of all of this, don't overlook the obvious value you provide—your clinical skills and expertise!

Clinical Expertise: In what ways do you stand out as a clinician? Do you have specialized training or experience in a particular area? Do you have a high success rate with a particular condition or have a unique approach to treatment? If so, these factors contribute to your Value Proposition. But don't worry if you don't have many clinical "extras" at the moment, nothing is set in stone. You can always fine-tune your Value Proposition as you gain more experience and learn what your patients want and need.

Proven Results: In what ways can you quantify the level of care you provide and the outcomes your patients experience? If you are offering evidence-based treatments and achieving positive outcomes, many patients will be willing to pay a premium for your services.

To be honest, I never could understand the quality measures that insurance companies tracked, because to me, in the end, the only person who should judge the quality of the care I provide is the patient in front of me. The one I'm actually treating.

The significance of your Value Proposition is rather simple: if you do quality work, if you provide a service equal in value to the amount you charge, then your patients will come back. If you don't, then they won't come back. It's pretty easy to figure that out.

Unique Selling Proposal (USP)

Your Value Proposition communicates all the ways in which you offer value to the patient. Your USP communicates all the ways in which your Value Proposition is unique and superior to that of your peers and competitors. It differentiates you from other practices.

Your Value Proposition convinces a prospective patient that your services are worth the amount you are charging. Your USP convinces a prospective patient that your Value Proposition is unique and can't be matched by any other practice.

A strong USP differentiates you from your competitors and helps you stand out as the ideal choice. It also helps you home in on niche markets that have not yet been identified and marketed to directly. Think of it as claiming "your slice of the pie." At the same time, understand that there are no limits to the number of slices in the pie. Pies grow as market needs are identified and businesses step up to meet those needs.

So, how do you develop a USP? Well, you go back to asking questions and you take a look at the answers. Be curious about your practice. Ask yourself what specific benefits does your practice offer that other practices don't?

- In what ways are the treatments and/or services you offer unique?

- In what ways is your approach to patient care unique?

- In what ways is your level of accessibility to patients unique?

As you answer these questions for yourself, begin thinking about how you will communicate these points effectively to your Target Market. Ask yourself questions like:

- What messaging will resonate with my Target Market?

- What channels of communication should I use to convey my USP?

- What language would best communicate my USP?

One of the ways I figured out my Value Proposition and my USP was rather simple: I talked to my existing patients. I asked them what I was doing well, and I asked them for suggestions for improvement. I asked them (if I could no longer practice) what they would look for in their next doctor. Having the time and the opportunity to interact with my patients like this was priceless. If you have the chance to do this in your current practice and with your current patient panel, take advantage of it!

Each practice is different, so each practice will have a different USP. However, Direct Care practices share a few unique qualities when compared to insurance-based practices. Here are some points you can include in your USP to communicate the advantages Direct Care Medicine has over insurance-based medicine

- *Personalized Care*: You provide patients with one-on-one care with the same doctor every visit.

- *Convenience*: It is easy for the patient to see you. You offer greater availability and accessibility through extended hours, telemedicine, and same-day appointments. You don't overbook your schedule, so your patients don't waste time in the waiting room.

- *Affordability*: You provide price transparency (no surprise billing), bundled pricing, and payment plans.

- *Quality Care*: You provide prompt and thorough diagnoses, effective treatments, and close patient follow-up.

- *Wellness Focus*: Your practice focuses on and promotes wellness through a proactive and comprehensive approach to healthcare, preventive care, and lifestyle coaching.

Brand

If I mention Coke™, Crest™, or Littman™, most of us immediately think of a soft drink, toothpaste, and our first stethoscope, respectively. That's the power of a brand. Each of those companies has managed to imbue a product with deep meaning and emotions and merge those feelings with the reputation of the company as a whole.

When it comes to marketing your Direct Care practice, YOU in essence are the product. Your Brand is your unique identity as a healthcare professional—your reputation as a physician. Building your Brand will be about defining who you are, what you stand for, and how you deliver care to your patients. This stands in stark contrast to the trend of commoditization in healthcare today with physicians being lumped into provider groups and labeled by medical license, DEA, or NPI. You, however, are a Direct Care physician. You have decided you are much more than a number! Thus, you need to build your Brand.

So, how do you stand out?

It's easier than you might think. You build a strong Brand by communicating a unique identity that resonates with your Target Market. Everyone has his or her own personal and professional story. That's where you start. With storytelling. The story of you as a person and as a physician.

Your story will communicate your values, your expertise, and your approach to patient care. It will showcase your strengths, highlight areas of specialization and convey the benefits you provide to your patients. Building your Brand through storytelling will create a sense of intimacy with your Target Market. A strong Brand will generate trust and loyalty among patients. This, in turn, will lead to return visits, referrals, and positive word-of-mouth advertising.

A strong Brand will help you elevate your market position and differentiate your practice from others. It can increase the perceived value of your services and allow you to raise your price point. As a Direct Care practitioner, you must regularly review your branding efforts and messaging. You must always make sure you are targeting the right patient population and communicating your value proposition effectively.

Creating Your Marketing Strategy

Now that you understand the marketing fundamentals (Target Market, Value Proposition, USP, and Brand), it's now time to bring all these things together and create a marketing strategy. As you create your marketing strategy, you need to plan and approach it methodically.

What you are marketing is YOU and your services. Your marketing strategy can choose to highlight different aspects of you and your services in different ways, at different times, and through different channels. Some of the different aspects I'm referring to include your product (that is you and the care you offer), your pricing (we will talk about this in-depth in the next chapter), your office (this is the location where you are working) and your distribution (this refers to how you are getting your target audience to find out about you and your practice).

A marketing strategy should be comprehensive. It should be implemented effectively, and it should constantly be monitored to see if its results are working.

The goal of your marketing strategy will be threefold:

- Attract new patients to your practice.

- Retain your existing patients.

- Build a strong reputation as a trusted medical professional.

Setting goals is a good start as these are the broad ideas that will define the overall direction and outcome that you want to achieve; however, as goals are the direction, outlining your objectives will give you the specific steps and targets to achieve those goals.

The Marketing Mix

The term marketing mix refers to the channels you will use to reach your target audience. Once you determine the channels, you want to plan out your marketing activities and schedule them in advance. This will help you stay organized and consistent with your messaging. Lastly, you want to create compelling content and information that will resonate and attract your target audience.

Patient Experience

Do not underestimate the power of office visits - not just from a clinical standpoint but from a marketing standpoint as well. Your patient's experience from the first encounter with scheduling, during check-in and triage, and with the actual examination through check-out will either leave the patient with a good feeling or not. You want to take care of their ailments and keep them healthy, but as a direct care doctor, you can do that unimpeded without interference which should be a contrast to the woes associated with traditional insurance-based models that many patients are used to experiencing in other office flows. Get into the habit of having your staff ask during checkout to ask for a review or referral. This is part of your marketing too. In my office, I ask for a review after the visit stating that "It is the greatest compliment to us to refer a family member or friend and it allows us to help more people."

Online Tactics

- *Create a website.* You want to develop a professional website that showcases you and your office. In today's world, setting up a practice website is a must-have for any private practice. Your practice's website is a crucial marketing channel where you can showcase your unique value proposition and services, provide information about your practice, and allow patients to schedule appointments online. You can also use your website to publish informative blog posts and other content that can attract and engage potential patients.

- *Utilize social media.* Social Media has revolutionized marketing in the last decade. Social media platforms like Facebook, Twitter, Instagram, and now, Reels and TikTok, are excellent channels to connect with potential patients, promote your practice, and share updates and news related to your practice. You can also use social media to build relationships with patients by sharing helpful health tips, promoting services, and engaging with followers by receiving feedback and answering questions.

- **_Implement Content Marketing._** In today's digital world, you need to develop a content marketing strategy that provides valuable information to patients and will position you as an authority in your field. This can come in the form of blog posts, videos, infographics, memes or shared articles, or related posts.

- **_Utilize Email Marketing._** Email marketing can be a highly effective way to communicate with patients and prospects, promote your services, and share news and updates related to your practice. You can use email marketing to send newsletters, appointment reminders, and special offers to your patients.

Referrals

Some patients come to your office because your message resonated with them directly; however, many others find your office indirectly through referrals. Take advantage of all your resources. Think of individuals who can serve as potential ambassadors for your practice. Word-of-mouth referrals are a powerful marketing tool, and you can incentivize your current patients to refer new patients to your practice by offering discounts or other rewards. You can also partner with other physicians, healthcare facilities, or complementary vendors and businesses to offer mutual referrals.

Advertising

Marketing and advertising are not the same thing - related, but distinct concepts. Advertising is a part of marketing that specifically refers to paid promotion or communication to your target audience.

Direct mail can be a targeted way to reach potential patients in your local area. You can use postcards, flyers, or other promotional materials to introduce your practice and services to people in your target demographic.

Online Advertising is different from social media channels. Google AdWords and social media advertising can be an effective way to target potential patients with your marketing messages. You can use these platforms to create targeted ads that appear to people searching for specific keywords or demographics.

Monitoring Your Efforts

When it comes to advertising, it is critical that as you implement, you monitor. As you follow your marketing plan and implement your tactics, keep track of the performance of your marketing efforts. This will help you identify what is working and what is not. Use the insights gained from monitoring your results to adjust your marketing tactics.

Measuring your performance can start with setting up tracking mechanisms. For example, use tools such as Google Analytics, social media insights, or email marketing metrics to track your results. Review your data and identify trends and patterns. Determine which marketing tactics are generating the best results. Use your data to make informed decisions about your marketing strategy. Continuously refine your approach to maximize your return on investment.

Once the initial goals of your new Direct Care practice have been achieved and you are well-established, remember, you cannot then rest on your laurels. It will be important for you to continually monitor and stay on track with attracting, maintaining, and sustaining a stream of patients into your practice to avoid stagnation.

CHAPTER 14

YOUR PRICING STRATEGY

At this point in your reading, I hope that you have a better understanding of how to run the business end of your practice and that your confidence is growing. With that said, I know you may be anxious for me to get to the issue of pricing. This is a topic that can feel rather mysterious to doctors who, generally speaking, have only ever relied on third-party systems to set their rates. It is true; pricing is one of the more challenging aspects of transitioning to Direct Care Medicine. However, my goal in this chapter is to remove the mystery and explain the methodology behind pricing.

As a Direct Care physician, **you will have no third-party setting your rates**. It will be between you and your patients. That might sound both liberating and frightening at the same time. And this can make many doctors incredibly uncomfortable. I get it! But let me be blunt here for a moment: you have to dig in and get past the discomfort. You must shift your mindset. It is imperative.

As you build your Direct Care private practice outside the traditional insurance-based model, pricing will be particularly important, because patients will be paying out-of-pocket for their healthcare. The price of a service can influence a patient's decision to choose one provider over another and can impact their overall satisfaction with the service they receive.

In my experience, I've identified a few preconceived notions doctors hold about pricing that are **flat-out wrong and must be corrected.**

- There exists one perfect price and the goal is to find it.

- Prices, once established, are written in stone.

- Someone else knows better than you do how to price your services.

- The best way to figure out pricing is through group consensus.

Throw all those ideas out of your head! They are not true!

Most of us like things to be clear-cut, black-and-white, yes-or-no, right or wrong. Unfortunately, when it comes to pricing, there will be no single answer, no one way to do things, no one-size-fits-all answer. But I'm not leaving you here. I will continue to help you shift your mindset away from these false notions about pricing and demonstrate a way for you to develop your unique pricing strategy. Once you figure out how to price your services correctly, you will not only survive in Direct Care Medicine; you will thrive!

A Small Detour

Allow me to take you on a small detour to help put things in perspective.

Have you ever hired a plumber to do work for you? Most of us have at some point. What do you remember about the experience? If you are anything like me, you felt relieved and grateful to have access to a professional who could solve your problem.

Our experiences with plumbers (and other professional service providers) offer us an opportunity to examine the issue of pricing from a different perspective. This can, in turn, provide valuable insight (light bulb moments) as you pursue your goal of creating a pricing strategy for your services. Follow along, as I take you through two hypothetical scenarios.

Imagine your garbage disposal starts making a horrific noise, metal on metal. It could be nothing more than a loose screw. Or—who knows? —maybe you need an entirely new disposal system. You call a plumber to come by and diagnose the problem and propose a solution, or better yet, several solutions at various price points for you to choose from. The plumber arrives over the next day or two, tightens the screw, or replaces the unit altogether, and you go back to stuffing banana peels down your sink.

Here's the second scenario. This one is more urgent. You wake up one Sunday morning and find a damp stain forming on the ceiling in your living room and a pocket of water building in the sheetrock directly above your family's heirloom baby grand piano. You need a plumber on the scene pronto. But it is Sunday, a day when most plumbers work on an emergency basis only and they charge off-hour rates. You quickly calculate the cost—both emotional and financial—of losing your piano and immediately accept the terms of Sunday plumbing services. The plumber arrives in time to find the source of the leak and save your piano. From that day on, you feel gratitude for that plumber every time you sit down and run your fingers along the keys.

Now imagine the exchange that takes place with the plumber in these two scenarios after he has diagnosed your problem and presented his solution or choice of solutions. Before he lifts a finger to fix anything, he first lets you know what the charge will be. At this point, the ball is in your court. You know what the problem is, what the stakes are, and what the cost will be to resolve the issue. You have all the information you need to decide if you want to move forward or decline his proposal. Or seek a second opinion.

Are you with me so far?

Ok, so now let me ask you this. How inappropriate would it be for you, in either of these situations, to flip the tables on the plumber and ask him why he thinks his services are worth so much, or why he is bringing up money when you are in such a vulnerable position? I think we'd all agree that would be very inappropriate. We all know that the plumber is running a business. We accept his right to set his rates and then let them be judged by market dynamics. After all, if the plumber wildly overprices his services, he won't be in business for very long. The only appropriate response is to accept or decline his services using your criteria for decision-making needs, perception of value, affordability, personal budget, etc.

Let's bring this back to our profession and try to figure out why we can't be more matter-of-fact about pricing (like plumbers). As doctors, we've been trained to provide care to the sick and infirm, to fight for our patient's lives, and to relieve suffering. For many of us, our work is more than a profession; it's a calling. The topic of money, by contrast, can feel awkward and unbecoming—or, in my own experience what I had been conditioned to think, kind of sleazy. No doctor wants to be thought of as "out to make a buck" off the suffering of others.

I am here to tell you that kind of thinking, while common in our profession, is neither fair nor correct. The fact of the matter is this: you are not a monk, and you haven't taken a vow of poverty. You have always been paid for your services. You've simply never been placed in the position of having to justify your pay to your patients. You've never had to market yourself or make a case for your value. Breaking free from the third-party payment system will require you to step up and do both.

As you do, keep in mind this: your patients aren't just patients. They are consumers—as we all are in various capacities—and as consumers, they engage (and pay for) the services of all kinds of professionals from plumbers to attorneys. The concept of paying for professional services is not foreign to any of us, even if we, as a society, have not yet become accustomed to applying the same type of calculations to healthcare services. This is now changing. People are beginning to recognize the value of their health in general and the value independent healthcare providers offer by helping them maintain or regain their health.

But now, here you are, taking steps to remove the third-party mediator from your relationship with your patients, and that leaves you, and only you, with the fundamental responsibilities of figuring out your rates and communicating them to your patients.

You can push this uncomfortable task out of your mind for only so long. The truth is, to move forward with your dream of breaking free from the old way of doing things, you will have to clear this crucial hurdle at some point.

Pricing Fundamentals

Pricing impacts EVERYTHING in your business. It impacts your marketing, your position in the marketplace, and your branding. It impacts your ability to attract, maintain and sustain patient flow in your practice. It impacts the sales and cash flow of your practice. Pricing ties all these elements of your business together. And changes in your pricing will ripple through each of these elements as well.

A good pricing strategy will consider all the factors that go into setting your prices. On the one hand, you need to charge enough for your services to cover expenses and make a profit. On the other hand, you need to make sure your prices are competitive and that your patients can afford your services. If you don't take the time to consider all factors, you could come up short one way or the other. If you underprice your services, you might fail to cover your expenses. Not good. If you overprice your services, you might struggle to attract patients. Also, not good. So, you see, it's a balancing act.

Before we get into the specifics of creating your pricing strategy, I must first go over a few basics.

What is the price?

Price is the amount of money that you (the seller) request and receive from the patient (the buyer) in exchange for services or goods (your care).

What is the pricing?

Pricing is the process of determining the value of your services. The price of your service will be reflective of its value and will also influence the consumer's perception of your service as being valuable. For example, if a doctor charged $100 for an appendectomy, what would you think about the value of this service? By pricing his service at $100, the doctor is communicating the value he places on his time, skills, and service, and, in this case, it's not very high. Here's another example: have you ever seen the same item being sold at completely different price points? Think cars. Did you notice how your perception of the item's value changed by its price?

What is a pricing strategy?

A pricing strategy is a plan for determining the prices a business will charge for its products or services. A well-designed pricing strategy can help a Direct Care practice attract, maintain and retain patients (your marketing goals), thereby ensuring that the practice remains financially sustainable. The goal is to set prices commensurate with the value of the care being provided but at the same time competitive enough to motivate patients to book appointments.

Some of the factors that you will want to consider when developing a pricing strategy include:

- The value of the service.

- The cost of providing the service.

- The level of patient demand for the service.

- The price being charged by competitors.

Why do we need a pricing strategy?

Without a pricing strategy, your efforts to price your services will be random and baseless. A pricing strategy, on the other hand, is just the opposite. It's focused and intentional. A pricing strategy considers multiple factors: the value of your services, the cost of providing your services, the demand for your services, and your competitors' prices for the same services. Without a strategy, your prices are likely to be out of alignment with one or more of these factors.

Ultimately, a successful pricing strategy for your Direct Care medical practice will depend on your ability to communicate the value of your services to patients and, in doing so, establish a strong reputation as a provider of high-quality, personalized healthcare. Recall your Value Proposition and Unique Selling Proposal (USP). By pricing your services appropriately and effectively communicating the value of those services to your Target Market, you will be able to attract, maintain and retain patients who are willing to pay for high-quality healthcare and, over time, you will be able to build a successful business. That's the goal!

What is the Relationship between Marketing and Pricing?

In the previous chapter, I told you that pricing plays a role in marketing. *In what way?* you may have wondered. Well, pricing impacts a patient's perception of you. Remember the hypothetical $100 appendectomy?

I'm not suggesting that you put any price you want on your services and patients will be convinced of the value. You can't convince patients that the value of your appendectomy is $1,000,000 simply by pricing it this way. You still have to consider other factors: demand for the service, the competitive landscape, and the economic demographics of your Target Market. Keeping all this in mind, pricing still comes down to perceived value.

And this is where your marketing strategy intersects with your pricing strategy. A successful marketing strategy will help your patients see the value of your services by explaining it to them and convincing them of it.

This is why you must spend time creating a strong Value Proposition and compelling USP. With the right marketing efforts—efforts that highlight the benefits of seeing a Direct Care physician and explaining the value of your service in particular—you can help patients feel more confident about your services and ultimately about the choice they make to see you.

For example, Direct Care Medicine offers one very clear advantage over insurance-based care: personalized attention from the doctor. The patient gets more time with the doctor and more personalized care from the doctor. Your marketing efforts must highlight this benefit to the patient. Most patients will recognize the value of this advantage. Those that do will then see the price of your services as being reflective of their value. The same goes for any specialized expertise you offer or unique services not available elsewhere. People will be able to appreciate the value of those benefits if you communicate it to them in your marketing.

With proper pricing and marketing of your services, you can establish yourself as a provider of high-quality, specialized medical care and a leader in the market. Patients who value the best possible healthcare for themselves will view your services as worth the investment of their money. You will become a stand-out leader in your field and attract the patients in your community who are willing to pay for the added value you provide.

Developing a Pricing Strategy

To create a successful pricing strategy, you must:

- Analyze the local market and your competition.

- Calculate the cost of providing your services.

- Fully embrace your Value Proposition.

- Assess your patient's ability to pay.

- Explore the various pricing models.

- Maintain competitive, transparent, and ethical standards.

Analyze the local market and your competition

You must familiarize yourself with the current market landscape in your area. What are the competitors in your healthcare space charging for similar services? What are patients willing to pay for these services? Answers to these questions can help you determine a competitive price range for your services.

Calculate the cost of providing your services

Knowing your KPIs never ceases to be important. This includes knowing the cost of providing your services. Keep in mind, calculating the cost of providing your services will take everything into account. It's a comprehensive calculation and should include all the costs associated with running your office. Your goal is to produce revenue that will exceed total expenses.

Fully embrace your Value Proposition

While it is important to consider the cost of providing services, it is also important to know and embrace your value as a physician and that of the services you are offering. Revisit your value proposition and USP to see how all the factors come together: convenience, customer service, and cost savings alongside your clinical skills. Taking the total package into account will help you to develop a pricing strategy that accurately reflects your value proposition. It will also allow you to be more highly compensated for your services.

Assess your patient's ability to pay.

You need to consider whether your target patient population can afford your services. Knowing the demographics and psychographics of your location can help assess your patient's ability to pay.

Explore the various pricing models.

There are several pricing model options for the Direct Care physician. That said, pricing models are typically dependent on your medical specialty and the type of services you are offering.

Your choice of pricing models includes:

- Pay-per-service.

- Flat Fee.

- Membership.

- Hourly Rates.

- Bundled Packages.

As a Direct Care physician, you are not limited to using only one type of pricing model in your practice. Most Direct Care practices use multiple models.

Many DPC practices use the membership model. However, given the episodic nature of care in DSC practices, they tend to rely upon a variety of pricing models in their business.

Although I did mention it in the list above, there is one pricing model I suggest you avoid. I do not recommend setting a price for your service based on an hourly rate. When physicians base their pricing solely on time, they can find themselves competing with the physicians out there who are willing to work longer hours at lower rates. This creates a race to the bottom, a situation in which physicians may feel pressured to work longer hours for less money to compete. And that diminishes the value of the service.

Pricing your services based on time will not be a profitable formula in the long term. Working according to a fixed hourly rate limits your income potential. How is that? Simple, time is a limited resource, therefore your income will be limited as well by that constraint. Not to mention the fact that the only way to increase your income when you are working on an hourly basis is to work more hours. And this can lead to burnout and a reduction in the quality of patient care. Does this sound familiar? Aren't those the reasons you are looking to escape to Direct Care medicine in the first place?

By contrast, pricing based on value can provide a more sustainable and profitable business model for you. When you focus on delivering high-quality care and when you strive toward improving patient outcomes, your Direct Care private practice can differentiate itself from other offices and attract patients who are willing to pay more for personalized, effective care. This can lead to increased revenue and profitability in the long term. When you price based on your Value Proposition and USP, you highlight the unique assets you as the physician bring to the table which are your knowledge and your skills. Never underestimate that! Remember: know your worth!

Maintain competitive, transparent, and ethical standards.

At this point, you now know you must consider the local market landscape, calculate the cost of providing your services, embrace your value, know your patients' ability to pay for your services and review the various pricing models to use in your practice. Taking these factors into consideration, you can now move forward with your pricing strategy. The final step is to make sure your pricing strategy remains competitive, transparent, and ethical. This is a hard and fast rule and should never be open to debate.

One of the hallmarks of Direct Care is price transparency. Guaranteeing price transparency means there are no hidden fees and no surprise billing for your services. Patients in this day and age have become accustomed to living with a big question mark over medical billing. It's a great source of anxiety for many. Price transparency, on the other hand, represents a breath of fresh air, a good night's sleep without worry. Price transparency is not for your sake, it is for your patients' sake. It allows them to make informed decisions. You maintain price transparency by publishing your fees on your website, or even better, by communicating the price to your patient in person before rendering care (remember the plumber). Contrast this experience with that of traditional insurance-based practices where no one knows the actual price of anything until claims are adjudicated.

Proof of Concept

So how do you know if you've created a rock-solid pricing strategy? How do you know if it's going to work? Honestly, you won't know if it will work in your particular market until you test it.

You can test your pricing strategy with a small group of patients to see if they are willing to pay the prices you've set for your services. Working with a small panel of patients will allow you to gain valuable patient insight and the opportunity to adjust your pricing based on their feedback.

Here are some ways Direct Care physicians can test their pricing:

- Offer a Promotion: Offer a discounted rate for the first 10 patients who sign up for a new service or package. This can help gauge patient interest and see if the pricing is competitive.

- Conduct Surveys: Communication with your patients is always insightful. Ask patients for feedback on the pricing of services and packages. This can help identify any concerns or objections patients may have and provide insights into how to adjust pricing.

- Monitor Patient Retention: Look at your patient volume after you set a new price and keep track of retention rates and feedback. If patients are not returning or are expressing dissatisfaction with pricing, it probably means that you need to adjust.

- Analyze Revenue and Expenses: You should always be monitoring your numbers. Review your revenue and expenses regularly to ensure that pricing is sustainable and profitable. If expenses are too high or revenue is too low, it may be necessary to adjust accordingly.

These are just a few examples of how you can test your pricing strategy with a small group of patients. Conducting these types of tests can help you determine if your pricing is competitive and if your patients are willing to pay for them. The results of these tests can also provide insight into how you might tweak prices to improve patient satisfaction and your profitability.

Theory versus Reality

Forget about medicine for a moment. If you owned a coffee shop, you would have to consider the cost of the coffee beans, milk, sugar, rent, salaries, etc., to determine what to charge for your coffee drinks. If the demand for coffee is high, you can charge a higher price, and conversely, if demand is low, you would reduce prices or find other ways to increase demand. The coffee shop may even conduct market research to find out what types of coffee drinks are popular in the area and set its prices accordingly.

In your medical practice, you will need to do the same thing. You will want to understand what your Target Market is looking for and what services they're willing to pay for. This information and insight will allow you to make an informed decision when setting your prices and ensure that your practice is successful and continues to grow.

Again, it's important to keep in mind that your prices aren't set in stone. If you find that your prices are too high or too low, you'll need to be flexible and make changes accordingly. If you charge too much, you might struggle to attract patients. And if you charge too little, you might not make enough money to keep your practice going in the long run. Have patience. This process may take time and require experimentation and adjustments along the way. The goal is to find the sweet spot: that point at which your prices accurately reflect both the value of your services and the amount your patients are able and willing to pay. Trust in the sweet spot and you will find it.

CHAPTER 15

YOUR TRANSITION STRATEGY

Now that you understand how to create a marketing strategy and a pricing strategy, it's time to pull everything together. Through careful planning and execution, you can successfully transition to a Direct Care practice. Keep in mind, however, that the process will be dynamic and fluid, and defined by your situation. It's important to remain flexible in terms of adjusting your strategy as you go along. Keep your eye on the KPIs of your practice and pace your steps according to the experience as it unfolds.

In this chapter, I've gathered a few pearls of wisdom to guide you along the path of transition. As I've mentioned a few times before, transitioning to Direct Care Medicine is a process. There is no magic formula or switch to flip. There will be easier days and there will be more challenging days. Stay the course, and you'll make it safely to the other side.

Communicate With Your Patients

It is important to communicate with your patients about your transition to a Direct Care practice. For them, your transition means cash pay and no more insurance. When you have your conversations (and they should be personal conversations), be sure to articulate your rationale for transitioning. Share your perspective but also point out what they stand to gain as well. In today's healthcare ecosystem, many patients have no idea what is going on behind the scenes.

It's been my experience that patients do want to understand what is happening from your point of view and why you feel you need to make the transition. I found my patients to be quite sympathetic. At the same time, they do need to know how the changes will impact them.

I was in private practice for 15 years before I began my transition, so I was fairly well-established with solid marketing strategies in place, consistently bringing in a steady flow of patients. However, pricing is part of marketing, so when pricing began to change, it impacted the dynamic I had going.

When that happened, I turned to my most reliable source for advice—my patients. I asked them how they made their decisions when selecting a doctor. I asked them why they chose to see me. I asked them for their thoughts and opinions about the changes in healthcare. In response, they shared their concerns with me.

This is what I mean by having a conversation. It starts by asking questions and being willing to listen to the answers. It was through these conversations that I learned what my patient's pain points were with the system. This feedback allowed me to make my transition about them as much as it was about me. Together, we learned how to transition my practice in a way that addressed my concerns as well as theirs.

When you have these conversations with your patients, be sure to highlight the benefits for them and the potential cost savings. Emphasize the importance of asking for the cash price from all the doctors they visit. It can be quite eye-opening to many!

Review Contracts as You Phase Out Insurance

In Section Three I walked you through the process of sorting out your insurance plans according to each one's impact on your revenue. I talked about the various factors to consider:

- The reimbursement rates per plan.

- Your overall patient volume per plan.

- The relative hassle and hidden cost per plan.

This sorting process will allow you to identify which plans are generating the most revenue for your practice and which plans are generating the least. With this information, you will be able to drop plans in an orderly manner, one that minimizes loss of revenue for your practice. Doing so will allow you to stay financially afloat as you build up the cash-based portion of your business.

However, before you drop any plans, you must first review your contracts with the insurance companies. You must thoroughly read through each contract to make sure you understand the termination policy—your responsibilities in particular. Your timeline for transitioning out of the insurance contracts and into a pure Direct Care practice will be shaped by your obligations under each contract. Most physicians phase out insurance payments gradually over a period of time.

Again, I cannot emphasize this enough: READ YOUR CONTRACTS carefully! And if you are contracted with federal (i.e., Medicare, Tricare, etc.) and state plans (i.e., Medicaid, etc.), be cognizant and careful not to violate any insurance laws while your contracts are in force. Talk to a healthcare insurance attorney if you have any specific questions.

Educate Your Staff on Billing and Collections

Your staff must be fully informed of your new business model and pricing schedule to minimize confusion, mixed messages, and clerical errors within the practice. Everyone in your practice must be on the same page regarding the new policies. You must all be relaying the same message to patients.

This will require you to train your staff on their new financial responsibilities regarding billing and collections. Every member of your staff that interacts with patients must be trained to collect payment in full at the end of each patient visit. Create scripts for your staff members to use when they explain the new model to patients—both in person and over the phone.

As you go through your transition away from insurance, patients might ask you to continue filing the claim for them. There are pros and cons to doing this. It might be a reasonable request to honor at the beginning of your transition; however, my recommendation is to cut all ties with the insurance companies you've dropped as soon as possible. Once you've collected payment from your patient at the end of the visit, the transaction is completed. I would recommend letting the patient file the claim with the insurance company and manage the reimbursement process on his own.

Follow Your Marketing Strategy

Have you created your marketing strategy yet? If so, you need to follow it. A well-defined Value Proposition and USP will clear a path for you forward as you transition. It is important for you to always highlight how your new business model has been designed to benefit your patients—both existing and new. You must communicate the value you have created for them by transitioning to Direct Care Medicine: increased access to care; greater individualized attention; cost savings. Articulating the pros of Direct Care Medicine and contrasting those pros with the cons of insurance-based healthcare will attract the kind of patients you want in your practice, the patients who share your values concerning their health, time, and money. Remember your goal is to attract, maintain and sustain patient flow. A well-crafted marketing strategy will keep you on track.

Focus On Your Target Market

Keep the focus on your patients—both your existing patients as well as potential new patients! Analyze your data. Continue doing your market research. Know your referral sources and target your advertising. Don't waste your time, energy, and money on anyone outside your Target Market. Focus your effort on people who need your services, want your services, and value your services. This is the population your practice exists to serve.

Follow Your Pricing Strategy

I am stating the obvious here, but you must follow your pricing strategy. Just like you must follow your marketing strategy. You now understand that a pricing strategy is based on the results of your market research. It's based on the preferences of your Target Market. There is empirical support for the pricing strategy. It's not random. And it never should be random.

That said, I'll add this caveat. You must remain vigilant when it comes to managing and updating the pricing strategy. Continue to 1) monitor costs and expenses, 2) remain aware of market supply and demand, 3) be mindful of your patient's perception of you and your office, and 4) watch your competition.

Manage Expectations and Be Prepared

Let me be straightforward: you WILL get resistance from both your staff and your patients. Be prepared! It always comes back to communication!

In the end, transitioning to a Direct Care practice requires careful planning and execution. By communicating with existing patients, reviewing contracts with insurance companies, educating staff, and following your marketing and pricing strategies, you can successfully make the switch to a third-party free Direct Care private practice!

CHAPTER 16

YOUR BUSINESS PLAN

Part of seeing a patient involves writing a progress note. At the end of each note, you include a treatment plan. Anyone who reviews the patient's chart can read your prescribed plan and know what protocol is being followed to treat the patient.

A business plan is similar to a treatment plan. It is a written explanation of your business strategy: your objectives and your plan for achieving those objectives. It includes an overview of your business's products and services, market position, financial projections, future goals, etc. A business plan can serve as a roadmap for you and for anyone else you allow to review your business. You might decide to seek funding through a business loan from a bank or you might bring another physician into the practice as a partner. These are two scenarios in which an outside party might ask to see the business plan for your practice.

A well-written business accomplishes the following:

- It clarifies the business goals for your practice.

- It assesses market demand for your services.

- It positions your practice for success.

- It allows you to make informed decisions about how to grow and manage your business.

A business plan is not meant to be a static document; it is a living document that should change as your practice grows and evolves. To keep your business on the path to success, you must commit to monitoring it regularly and making necessary changes. When you do make changes, you will want to update your business plan to keep it current at all times.

A good business plan will include the following key components:

- Executive Summary

- Company Description

- Market Analysis

- Pricing Strategy

- Marketing Strategy

- Financial Projections

- Plan of Operations

I recommend you also include a Mission Statement in your business plan, even though I haven't seen that many in the physician business plans I have reviewed. Going through the exercise of writing a Mission Statement for your business helps ground you in the purpose of your practice. Over the years, it is easy to get mired in the daily minutia of running your business and lose touch with the greater meaning of it all. Include a Mission statement in your business plan and you review it along with your business operations regularly. You won't regret doing so. It will help you stay connected with your core values and maintain a principled mindset as a Direct Care practitioner.

Let's now look at the various components of a business plan in greater detail.

Executive Summary

The Executive Summary is the short version of your business plan. Kind of like a *Cliffs Notes* version. It provides a brief overview of the larger plan, highlighting key points and statistics such as your value proposition, goals, and financial projections. It should also include funding needs if that is an issue.

I recommend writing your Executive Summary last–after you finish writing your entire business plan from start to finish. You want the Executive Summary to be truly reflective of the fully finalized business plan. That will be hard to do if it's the first part of the plan you write. When you do write your Executive Summary, keep it succinct and compelling. It should grab your reader's attention and make it very clear who you are and what your practice is all about.

Company Description

The Company Description describes your business operations in full. As a Direct Care private practice, you will include a list of your services and products and a profile of your Target Market. Be sure to include patient visits, treatments, procedures, and surgeries. You can also share with the reader the conditions you treat, as well as any special programs you offer such as preventative care, lifestyle medicine, and nutritional counseling.

When you describe your Target Market, include as many details as possible: age, income bracket, physical location, and personal philosophies. Be sure to highlight the fact that your patients are seeking healthcare outside the traditional insurance model, that they place a high priority on maintaining their health, and that they value services that help them achieve their health goals.

This section is also an ideal place to explain to the reader how your business is structured legally. Where is your business registered? What is its legal structure? Who are the officers and what are their roles? These are the kind of questions you should ask.

Market Analysis

This section will provide an in-depth analysis of your Target Market, including the demographic and psychographic data, the local market trends, and a competitive profile of your area. Be sure to identify potential market opportunities as well as any realistic challenges your practice is facing. Before writing your Market Analysis, you should revisit your Value Proposition and USP.

The information you include in this section should demonstrate that you have done your due diligence regarding market research. You must show that you understand the healthcare arena as it pertains to the community you serve. You must explain why you chose to build a Direct Care practice as an alternative to the traditional insurance-based model. You will want to highlight the advantages your practice offers over other competitors in the area—your USP. Don't forget to hammer home the many advantages to patients of Direct Care Medicine as opposed to insurance-based care.

Pricing Strategy

The Pricing Strategy and Marketing Strategy are often combined into one section in the business plan. However, given the unique nature of each physician's private practice, I believe the Pricing Strategy should be a separate section in your business plan. Services vary widely from one practice to the next. Even for a single service, there can be a wide range of differentiation in terms of specifics. Take the *patient visit* for example, it can be a visit in the office, at home, via telemedicine, or in a facility. You can provide as much or as little information in this section depending on who will be reviewing the business plan. You can provide a summary of your pricing strategy, or you can go into great detail. It's your choice.

As you write this section, refer back to the Pricing Strategy chapter and review the connection between pricing and value. Be sure to explain the value Direct Care Medicine offers patients. Not everyone who reads your business plan will understand that, so you must be prepared to address any concerns or biases the reader might have about a cash-based private practice. Assure the reader that your pricing strategy is driven by the value of your products and services as well as the Direct Care model of your practice.

Marketing Strategy

This section details your strategy, including tactics and channels, for promoting your practice and attracting new patients. Be sure to include your social media activities and referral process.

As you write this section, make sure you answer the following questions:

1. What is your strategy for finding new patients?

2. How will you promote your services to your patients and your referral sources?

3. How will you position yourself as the ideal choice for patients seeking help?

4. How will you convince patients to make an appointment to see you?

You can generalize or be as specific as you want when answering these questions. But they should all be addressed to some extent.

Financial Plan

In this section, you will provide financial forecasts for revenue, expenses, profit margins, and cash flow. You must explain how your business will earn revenue and how it's going to make a profit off that revenue. You want to demonstrate that your business will be sustainable. If you have plans to expand and scale up your business, include them in this section.

Any funding requirements or investment needs should be included in this section. If you do have a funding request, you must be specific about the details. Why do you need the funds? What repayment terms are you considering?

Plan of Operations

This section should detail the day-to-day operations of your practice, including staffing, scheduling, and administrative processes.

I would write this out in three paragraphs. In the first paragraph, I would talk about how the office will look from the patient's perspective. You don't necessarily have to be specific, but you want to give the highlights of the patient experience.

In the second paragraph, you will want to mention how the back end of the office functions, primarily the clinical aspects. Now in this section, you can be more specific. This is where you will mention the roles that each of your staff members performs. Don't forget to mention you and your role as the main physician.

In the last paragraph, this is where you will highlight the administration end of things and your role as owner. Include things that have to be done to ensure long-term stability and smooth operations.

Finally, although there is not typically a section called Conclusion, I would recommend that your last page ties everything together and summarizes the key points of your business plan. It should emphasize the strengths and advantages of having a Direct Care medical practice and why your practice is expected to succeed.

Your business plan will likely be read at some point, by an individual or individuals in a position to assist you. For this reason, you want to provide as clear a picture of your business as possible, so that they can make a well-informed decision.

Writing a comprehensive business plan is one of the most important steps in launching a successful business. It helps articulate your mission, allows you to set achievable goals, helps you identify and focus on your Target Market and develop a strong Marketing Strategy. By taking the time to write a thoughtful business plan, just like you would when you write a logical treatment plan for your patient, the success, health, and growth of your practice will be rooted in a firm foundation. Your business plan will serve as the framework with which you can start building your practice. It will also serve as a starting benchmark that can be used as a reference as you assess and reassess your business each year.

CONCLUSION

"You never change things by fighting the existing reality. To change something, build a new model that makes the existing model obsolete."
- Buckminster Fuller, architect, systems theorist, writer, designer, inventor, and futurist.

Congratulations!

You are now set to soar!

Whether you're a new doctor or a seasoned physician, I hope that you have found this book to be a guide to help you navigate the uncharted territory of creating a successful private practice that is third-party-free.

I wrote this book to help physicians learn to thrive in private practice in today's healthcare arena. I wrote this to empower you, the physician, to be intentional in your thinking and decision-making as you map out a cohesive plan to build your own Direct Care private practice.

Physician burnout is real. I was able to find a way to escape my burnout in private practice by going third-party payor free and did it without changing the way I practice but by changing the way I interact with the system.

First Do No Harm is a tenet that we practice clinically with our patients, but doctors need to learn to practice this for themselves. I believe that this involves untethering themselves from third-party payors. We want doctors to stay in medicine, and we want to attract good people to go into medicine.

Transitioning from an insurance-based practice to a cash-based practice can be a significant change for both physicians and patients. IT IS NOT EASY! If it was, everyone would do it! You will have to work and work to build this, but IT IS WORTH IT!

As you can see, there is not one way to do things, but there is a way you can transition out of the traditional insurance-based practice into a Direct Care Private Practice.

I hope that I have given you the insight to see a different perspective and a different approach to the problem.

What does Direct Care look like in my office?

My Direct Care practice is ACCESSIBLE

You don't need a referral to see me, even if I'm a specialist. There is no checking for in-network, no authorization for referral. We tell the referring physician, if you want me to see your patient, send the referral and we'll explain to them what we can do *and let your patient decide!*

ANYONE can come in and see me, whether you have insurance or not – there are no network restrictions.

My Direct Care practice is AFFORDABLE

My prices are all listed and quoted to the patient before we do any procedure; we allow our patient to have an informed decision. This is true for office visits, for procedures, including surgeries - both in the office and outpatient.

Most of my patients have insurance and some can get reimbursed for their care. At the end of the visit, we can give our patients a receipt of what they have paid for services. If they have a third-party payor, they would like to request reimbursement from – go for it!

My Direct Care practice is AVAILABLE

There are fewer discrepancies in the care that I want to offer and give my patients because there is no third-party intermediary that needs to be consulted to deem my treatment, my prescription, or my request for a test as being medically necessary.

There is less inefficiency in my office because removing the third-party payor creates a more fluid office flow and my staff is not wasting time filing claims or waiting on the phone for a representative. And as a clinician, I can focus on actual patient care; because I have the time during the visit and can write a progress note that is succinct and relevant -- and not on a predetermined template in the electronic medical record that will prompt with bullet points to comply with diagnosis codes so that we get paid for the office visit, treatment or procedure.

As for emergent concerns, my patient just calls our office and is triaged by someone they know and reassured that in many instances. They can be in town or out of town. If the situation ends up being something that we can handle, it can be managed via phone, through telemedicine, or with a visit to the office and it bypasses the unnecessary need to make a trip to urgent care or the emergency room.

The pandemic resulted in showing the benefits of **my Direct Care practice that can be ADAPTABLE.**

When everything else shut down in March 2020, Direct Care practices were still functioning because we stayed in contact with our patients. Telemedicine was not a new concept and remains an active part of Direct Care.

Remember, patients are treated by doctors, not insurance. Patients CAN go to doctors directly and Doctors CAN treat patients directly. When this happens, doctors can do their job and do it better without interference. Patients get better care.

It's care that can be focused on prevention. It's proactive rather than reactive. It becomes affordable because there are no other players in the mix. Price transparency results in no surprise charges.

Direct Care practices allow CONTINUITY OF CARE!

So, consider the following next steps -

Write your business plan. To do this well, you will have to incorporate everything that we have discussed, and the more detailed you are, the more insight you will have to make better decisions and choices. Be methodical with S.M.A.R.T. goals that are specific, measurable, attainable, relevant, and time-based (so that you have a deadline).

Implement your Plan. Once you have created your plan, it's time to put it into action - now, the *rubber meets the road*. Identify and prioritize your steps and remember to track your progress. Keep a journal.

Monitor your Results. Keep track of your results, particularly marketing and pricing strategy. Analyze your data regularly to see what is working and what is not. Adjust accordingly.

Know when to Get Help. If you feel overwhelmed or struggling, there is no shame in seeking assistance. Someone has already traveled a similar path. The beauty about those in Direct Care, everyone wants it to work and for everyone to succeed because in the end, we all benefit.

Stay Committed. Once you have done the market research, know your target audience, have created your marketing and pricing strategies, and have written your business plan, you will stay on course and follow your goals and objectives. Persistence and dedication will prevail.

Your road ahead may have its challenges, but it's through overcoming those hurdles that you'll emerge stronger and more fulfilled in your personal and professional journey.

The *See One, Do One, Teach One* pedagogy works, but we need to show them the way!

SHARE THIS BOOK WITH OTHERS!

As you continue along, know that you have so many fellow colleagues rooting for you to succeed.

I'll be one of them! Just reach out!

You've Got This!!!!

A GROWING MOVEMENT

As physicians, continuing to practice in a system that is controlled by third parties and doesn't value the doctor-patient relationship is bad both for doctors and patients. Things will only get worse as long as we are compliant.

Daniel Paul, MD - Orthopedic Surgery
Owner/Founder, Easy Orthopedics

The Medical Profession has been decimated by a number of forces that systematically destroyed physician autonomy and critical thinking. These include the third-party payment system, so-called "evidence-based medicine," payment for performance schemes, and electronic charting. Faced with declining payments and increased costs, many doctors fled private practice to become employees in large corporate systems. It is fundamentally impossible to practice high quality, ethical, and scientific medicine in such a setting. The only hope for ethical physicians is in direct pay, third-party free, independent private practice.

Richard Amerling, MD - Nephrology
Chief Academic Officer, The Wellness Company

Understanding and leveraging entrepreneurship is one of the key concepts to taking back the field of medicine. It is crucial, now more than ever, for doctors everywhere to exercise entrepreneurial prowess so that they're, once again, in the "driver's seat";for the sake of not only their own well-being, but their patients and the sacred healthcare relationship.

Dana Coriel, MD - Internal Medicine
Founder & CEO, Doctors on Social Media

There's another life waiting for you in Direct Care. A place where doctors can be doctors, patients are getting better, and everyone is happy. I want all of my friends and colleagues to enjoy a life that they've worked so hard for and Direct Care offers that freedom.

Tea Nguyen, DPM - Podiatry
Owner/Founder, Pacific Point Podiatry
Host, *The Direct Care Way* Podcast

Today, physicians who are hospital employed or are part of a large network are forced to see increasing numbers of patients in a limited amount of time in order to be lucrative for the system. This model risks medical errors, and many patients feel that their needs are not being met. The Direct Care model allows the physician to spend more time with each individual patient to provide better patient outcomes and health. Eliminating insurance billing and administrative costs results in cost savings for patients. This is the definition of individualized, personalized patient care.

Hania Bednarski, DO - Oncoplastic Breast Surgery
Owner/Founder, Serenity Surgery

When my grandfather George Edward Legg, MD was accepted to medical school in 1937, a family friend, J. Harris Brown, MD, sent him a letter and told him this "Your life shall never be entirely your own, but there will be many things that will make you forget the hardships and your heart [will be] happy for the good that you will do for humanity." Fast forward nearly a century later and those inspiring words were fading. Morally conflicted between my Hippocratic Oath and the third parties forcefully interfering with how I can provide care for my patients, the words of my Oath began to fade too. I now practice family medicine using the DPC model and with a pure patient-physician relationship. DPC allows me to be the best physician possible for my patients. I think back to those words shared with my grandfather – what sage advice and so profound nearly 90 years later. If you believe that too and want the same, you must create that for your patients and for yourself. It's worth fighting for!

Kimberly Legg Corba, DO - Family Medicine
Owner/Founder, Green Hills Direct Family Care

RESOURCES

PHYSICIAN ORGANIZATIONS FOR DIRECT CARE

American Association of Physicians & Surgeons
Direct Primary Care Alliance / DPC Alliance
Direct Specialty Care Alliance / DSC Alliance
Docs4Patient Care
DPC Action
DPC Frontier
Benjamin Rush Institute

SUPPORTING DIRECT CARE

Free Market Medical Association
Freedom Healthworks
Hint Health
Green Imaging
Mitigate Partners
Surgery Center of Oklahoma
Wellbridge Surgical

PROMOTING DIRECT CARE

My DPC Story Podcast
The Direct Care Way Podcast
The EntreMD Podcast
The Podcast by KevinMD
Cash Patient Free Market Podcast
Healthcare Americana Podcast
Doctors on Social Media | SoMeDocs

ACKNOWLEDGEMENTS

In addition to my husband and children, I want to thank my parents, known to many simply as Drs. Dewey and Adelaide, who by their example demonstrated the epitome of what doctoring should be and how to prioritize patient-centric care at the same time balance family life. Thank you too to my Aunt Elsa, for teaching me the solid business foundations she incorporated in the management of my parents' office - many processes that I still incorporate into my own practice today.

To Susan (Shippey) Patnaik, my editor, a big THANK YOU for helping me turn the idea of this book into a reality. How fortuitous it was to reconnect again, and the timing could not have been more serendipitous that we would work on a project like this! I thank you for your thoughtful guidance in helping me shape this manuscript into something that I am very proud of sharing. I think our common ground having grown up in Pensacola, remembering the way medicine used to be, and how our physician parents interacted and approached their profession, gave you an added insight that allowed you to truly understand what I wanted to say and help me transform my vision into words!

To my beta readers - Ann Bollert, Lisa Smith, Robyn Rease and Jason Tindall who offered their precious time and honest feedback. Your diverse perspectives and constructive criticism were invaluable in shaping the final form of this book.

To my incredible office staff, Adam Rogers and Gloria Thomas, who rode the transition journey with me. It was not just about staying financially afloat while maintaining the quality of care, but you both embraced the shift with patience, understanding, and compassion. I credit our patients transitioning with us as a demonstration of trust that together our office has built through the years.

To my dear patients, for inspiring me to write this. Each day, I am humbled and honored that you entrust me with your care, but your coaxing, encouragement, and support has been instrumental in allowing me to pursue both my passions and my profession.

Lastly, a big thank you to you - yes, YOU, the reader! Your interest in my work is the ultimate reward for my efforts. Your belief in me inspires my belief that there are others out there that believe that there is a way to reclaim physician autonomy and restore the doctor-patient relationship!

ABOUT THE AUTHOR

Dr. Grace Torres-Hodges is a board-certified podiatrist and foot surgeon who has been serving the communities of Northwest Florida and South Alabama since 2001.

Dr. Torres-Hodges completed her undergraduate studies at Vanderbilt University, received her Doctor of Podiatric Medicine degree from the New York College of Podiatric Medicine, and received a Masters in Business Administration from the Quantic School of Business & Technology. She completed her post-graduate residency training in podiatric medicine and surgery at St. Vincent's Medical Center.

Dr. Torres-Hodges has shared her knowledge with the next generation of physicians through the DPM Mentor Network and as adjunct faculty at Florida State University College of Medicine and the USUHS programs at Eglin Air Force Base and Navy Hospital Pensacola.

She has been a featured speaker for Get Healthy Pensacola and offers insights into foot health articles that have been featured in Real Simple, Good Housekeeping, Family Circle, and Prevention Magazine, as well as in interviews with the Wall Street Journal and National Public Radio. Dr. Torres-Hodges is a recipient of the FPMA Physician of the Year Award and has been recognized as a US Top Doctor by HealthTap.

Made in the USA
Columbia, SC
13 February 2025

53668412R00122